SUPER EASY CARNIVORE DIET COOKBOOK FOR BEGINNERS

THE COMPLETE GUIDE TO HIGH PROTEIN EATING FOR INFLAMMATION RELIEF, AUTOIMMUNE SUPPORT AND MENTAL CLARITY - INCLUDES 100+ SIMPLE RECIPES, 30-DAY MEAL PLAN & SHOPPING LISTS

ERIN GARTEN

© Copyright 2025 – Erin Garten. All rights reserved.
Published by Kwon Royalty Publishing, under its Tasty Shelf imprint.
No part of this book may be reproduced, distributed, or transmitted in any form or by any means, including photocopying, recording, or other electronic or mechanical methods, without the prior written permission of the publisher, except in the case of brief quotations used in book reviews and certain other non-commercial uses permitted by copyright law.

Legal Notice:
This book is copyright protected. It is only for personal use. You cannot amend, distribute, sell, use, quote or paraphrase any part, or the content within this book, without the consent of the author or publisher.

Disclaimer Notice:
Please note the information contained within this document is for educational and entertainment purposes only. All effort has been executed to present accurate, up to date, reliable, complete information. No warranties of any kind are declared or implied. Readers acknowledge that the author is not engaged in the rendering of legal, financial, medical or professional advice. The content within this book has been derived from various sources. Please consult a licensed professional before attempting any techniques outlined in this book.

By reading this document, the reader agrees that under no circumstances is the author responsible for any losses, direct or indirect, that are incurred as a result of the use of the information contained within this document, including, but not limited to, errors, omissions, or inaccuracies.

Table Of Contents

Introduction 6
Carnivore Diet History 8
Getting Started With The Carnivore Diet 10

Breakfast 12
Carnivore Breakfast Sausage Patties 13
Carnivore Omelet With Ground Beef 14
Smoked Salmon And Scrambled Eggs 15
Lamb Chop Breakfast Platter 16
Beef Fat-Fried Chicken Thighs 17
Beef Tallow-Fried Eggs 18
Creamy Scrambled Eggs 19
Butter-Basted Salmon Bites 20
Easy Salmon Patties 21
Duck Eggs And Crispy Bacon 22
Poached Eggs With Bone Broth Sauce 23
Egg And Cream Cheese Pancake 24
Baked Eggs In Bone Broth 25
Grilled Sausage With Fried Duck Egg 26
Seared Beef Heart With Buttered Eggs 27

Lunch 28
Grilled Ribeye With Garlic Butter 29
Pan-Seared Salmon With Lemon Butter 30
Pork Chops With Crispy Cracklings 31
Lamb Shank Stew 32
Smoked Brisket With Bone Broth Glaze 33
Roasted Chicken Wings With Beef Fat Drizzle ... 34
Butter-Poached Duck Legs 35
Bone Broth-Braised Lamb Ribs 36
Grilled Sausage And Butter Dip 37
Beef Tenderloin And Bone Marrow Plate 38
Pan-Fried Pork Cutlets With Duck Fat 39
Crab Meat With Garlic Butter Sauce 40
Lamb Ribs With Herb-Infused Butter 41
Crispy Duck Wings With Tallow Dip 42
Seared Cod With Beef Fat Sauce 43

Dinner 44
Slow-Cooked Beef Short Ribs 45
Roast Leg Of Lamb With Pan Juices 46
Pork Loin With Butter Herb Glaze 47
Grilled Salmon With Crispy Skin 48
Whole Roasted Chicken With Tallow Rub 49
Duck Confit With Crispy Skin 50
Pan-Seared Scallops With Butter 51
Grilled Swordfish With Bone Marrow Butter 52
Slow-Roasted Lamb Shoulder 53
Venison Roast With Garlic Butter Sauce 54
Lamb Meatballs In Bone Broth Sauce 55
Pork Belly Roast With Crackling Crust 56
Grilled Lobster With Butter Dipping Sauce 57
Braised Oxtail In Beef Stock 58
Filet Mignon With Duck Fat Gravy 59

Snacks & Small Bites 60
Chewy Pork Rind Bites 61
Bacon-Wrapped Cheese Sticks 62
Hard-Boiled Eggs With Salted Butter 63
Carnivore Egg Muffins 64
Lamb Meatballs With Beef Fat Drizzle 65
Smoked Salmon Rolls With Cream Cheese 66
Grilled Shrimp Skewers With Garlic Butter 67
Carnivore-Style Deviled Eggs 68
Pan-Fried Sausage Bites 69
Pork Belly Crisps With Beef Fat Glaze 70

Soups & Broths 71
Beef Bone Broth Soup 72
Creamy Chicken And Egg Drop Soup 73
Lamb Shank And Bone Marrow Stew 74
Shrimp And Crab Bisque (Dairy Optional) 75
Spiced Duck Broth With Egg Yolk Swirls 76
Slow-Cooked Oxtail Soup 77
Creamy Salmon Chowder 78
Roasted Bone Marrow And Garlic Soup 79
Pork Belly Soup With Crispy Fat Topping 80
Lobster Bisque With Creamy Butter Base 81

Appetizers & Starters 82
Seared Scallops In Garlic Butter 83
Carnivore Meatballs 84
Butter-Fried Chicken Livers 85
Smoked Salmon Bites With Cream Cheese 86
Crispy Chicken Wings With Butter Dip 87
Grilled Shrimp Skewers In Herb Butter 88
Bacon-Wrapped Cheese Bites (Optional Dairy) 89

Fried Pork Belly Cubes With Garlic Butter 90
Grilled Lamb Chops With Mint Butter 91
Crispy Duck Breast Bites With Savory Glaze 92

Side Dishes 93
Bacon-Wrapped Sausage Bites 94
Butter-Roasted Chicken Thighs 95
Grilled Chicken Tenders 96
Pork Belly Strips With Herb Butter Glaze 97
Beef Steak Bites 98
Pan-Seared Lamb Chops With Garlic Butter 99
Grilled Salmon With Bone Broth Reduction 100
Scrambled Egg And Pork Belly Mix 101
Butter-Basted Scallops As A Side Dish 102
Crispy Chicken Fat Bites 103

Desserts 104
Egg Custard With Heavy Cream 105
Whipped Cream Cheese Mousse 106
Carnivore Panna Cotta 107
Frozen Butter Bites With Vanilla Flavoring 108
Creamy Egg Pudding 109
Keto Carnivore Ice Cream 110
Cream Cheese And Egg Soufflé 111
Carnivore Chocolate Mousse 112
Salted Caramel Egg Custard 113
Salted Butter Fudge 114

Drinks 115
Bone Broth Latte With Butter 116
Whipped Cream Coffee 117
Salted Beef Tea (Warm Broth Drink) 118
Carnivore Milkshake 119
Carnivore Bulletproof Coffee 120

Shopping List 121
1st Week Meal Plan 122
2nd Week Meal Plan 123
3rd Week Meal Plan 124
4th Week Meal Plan 125

Conclusion 126

INTRODUCTION

The Super Easy Carnivore Diet Cookbook for Beginners serves as your comprehensive guide to transforming your health through high-protein eating. Drawing inspiration from Jordan Peterson's widely-shared success story, this cookbook demonstrates how a meat-based diet can help reduce inflammation, support autoimmune conditions, and enhance mental clarity.

With over 100 simple recipes, this cookbook prioritizes both nutrition and practicality, offering meals that can be prepared quickly using readily available ingredients. From energizing breakfasts to satisfying dinners, each recipe has been carefully crafted to deliver the full benefits of the carnivore diet while keeping preparation straightforward and manageable for beginners.

The included 30-day meal plan eliminates guesswork by providing a structured approach to establishing new eating habits. Accompanied by detailed weekly shopping lists, this system makes grocery shopping efficient and stress-free, allowing you to focus on your health journey rather than complex meal planning.

The cookbook specifically addresses three key areas where the carnivore diet has shown particular promise: inflammation management, autoimmune support, and mental clarity enhancement. You'll learn how to select quality proteins, prepare them for maximum nutritional benefit, and create satisfying meals that support your body's natural healing processes.

Whether you're dealing with chronic inflammation, autoimmune issues, brain fog, or simply seeking a clearer, more focused mind, this cookbook provides the practical tools and knowledge needed for success. By combining ancient wisdom with modern understanding, these beginner-friendly recipes and guidelines will help you achieve optimal wellbeing through the power of high-protein eating.

CARNIVORE DIET HISTORY

For thousands of years, humans thrived as hunters, gatherers, and providers. Long before the advent of agriculture, our ancestors relied on what nature had to offer in its purest form—meat. The carnivore diet isn't just a trendy lifestyle; it's a return to the primal roots that sustained our species for millennia.

From the earliest days of human history, survival was centered around securing nutrient-dense, energy-rich food sources. The tools our ancestors crafted were designed not for farming, but for hunting—sharp spears and arrows meant to bring down bison, deer, and other game. These hunting practices weren't just about sustenance; they laid the groundwork for communities to form, for collaboration and innovation to thrive. Meat wasn't just a meal—it was life itself.

As human migration expanded across continents, regional variations in meat-based diets began to emerge. Arctic peoples like the Inuit relied almost exclusively on fish, seal, and whale for sustenance. In the African savannahs, tribes like the Maasai built their diets around cattle. These groups thrived on what many today might consider restrictive eating patterns, but their health, vitality, and longevity told a different story.

Over time, the advent of agriculture shifted humanity's focus toward grains, fruits, and vegetables. While this transition helped populations grow, it also introduced chronic illnesses and nutritional deficiencies previously unheard of in primarily meat-eating societies. Ancient texts from the Greeks and Romans began to document the impact of these new dietary shifts, highlighting a divide between wealthier classes who consumed refined grains and poorer communities who relied more on whole foods, including meats.

Fast forward to the 20th century, and the meat-centric diet started to fade from favor amidst the rise of processed foods, industrial farming, and an overemphasis on carbohydrates. However, as chronic diseases like obesity, diabetes, and heart issues surged, questions arose about whether humanity had drifted too far from its evolutionary diet.

Enter the modern resurgence of the carnivore diet. Vilhjalmur Stefansson, an Arctic explorer in the early 1900s, documented his experience living among the Inuit, subsisting entirely on fish and meat while maintaining exceptional health. Decades later, in the 21st century, pioneers like Dr. Shawn Baker and Dr. Paul Saladino brought the carnivore diet back into the spotlight, championing its potential for reversing chronic illnesses and restoring vitality.

A particularly influential figure in popularizing the carnivore diet was Jordan Peterson, the renowned clinical psychologist and author. In 2018, Peterson shared his experience with the diet, describing how it helped him manage severe health issues, including depression and autoimmune symptoms. His daughter, Mikhaila Peterson, had introduced him to the diet after her own successful experience using it to address various health conditions. Jordan Peterson's public discussion of his dramatic health improvements on the carnivore diet—including better mental clarity, weight management, and reduced inflammation—helped bring this dietary approach into mainstream conversation and sparked wider interest in its potential benefits, particularly for mental health.

Today, the carnivore diet has become more than a niche lifestyle—it's a movement. With growing communities online, countless success stories, and scientific studies exploring its benefits, this diet challenges conventional wisdom about what it means to eat healthily. The testimonials of figures like Jordan Peterson have helped bridge the gap between ancient wisdom and modern application, showing how this primal approach to nutrition can address contemporary health challenges.

By looking back at our ancestors and embracing the nutrient-packed simplicity of a meat-based diet, the carnivore lifestyle offers a path not just to survival, but to thriving in a modern world full of dietary distractions. This book is your invitation to rediscover that path. Whether you're curious about the science, drawn to its simplicity, or simply looking for a way to feel your best, the carnivore diet connects you with the primal wisdom that fueled humanity for generations.

GETTING STARTED WITH THE CARNIVORE DIET

Adopting the carnivore diet can feel like stepping into uncharted territory, but it's rooted in a simple and straightforward philosophy: nourish your body with animal-based foods that offer maximum nutrition with minimal effort. This chapter will guide you through what the carnivore diet is, the benefits you can expect, and how to navigate the challenges that may arise along the way.

What Is the Carnivore Diet?
At its core, the carnivore diet is exactly what it sounds like—a diet centered on consuming animal-based foods. It is a return to the ancestral eating patterns of our hunter-gatherer forebears, designed to fuel the body with nutrient-dense, highly bioavailable foods.

The key principles are simple:
1. Focus on animal products such as meat, fish, eggs, and animal fats.
2. Eliminate all plant-based foods, including fruits, vegetables, grains, and legumes.

What's Allowed?
- **Meats:** Beef, pork, lamb, chicken, duck, and other animal proteins.
- **Seafood:** Fish and shellfish like salmon, shrimp, and scallops.
- **Eggs:** A versatile staple, perfect for quick meals.
- **Fats:** Butter, tallow, lard, ghee, and suet.
- **Other:** Bone broth, organ meats (liver, heart, kidneys), and minimal dairy (if tolerated).

What's Excluded?
- Fruits, vegetables, grains, and legumes.
- Sugars, sweeteners, and processed foods.
- Vegetable oils and seed oils.

There are different levels of adherence to the carnivore diet:
- **Strict Carnivore:** Focuses solely on animal-based foods with no exceptions.
- **Keto-Carnivore:** Allows for minimal non-carnivore additions like herbs, spices, or small amounts of dairy.
- **Flexible Carnivore:** Includes occasional plant-based foods like coffee, tea, or seasonings to ease the transition.

Whether you choose strict or flexible carnivore, the key is finding a version of the diet that works for your goals and lifestyle.

Benefits and What to Expect
One of the most exciting aspects of the carnivore diet is its potential to transform your health and well-being.

Potential Benefits
- **Weight Loss:** By eliminating carbohydrates, the body shifts into fat-burning mode, which helps with shedding excess weight.
- **Improved Energy:** A steady intake of fats and proteins provides long-lasting energy without the crashes associated with carb-heavy diets.
- **Mental Clarity:** Many report enhanced focus and reduced brain fog, thanks to stable blood sugar levels.
- **Reduced Inflammation:** The elimination of potentially inflammatory plant compounds may alleviate joint pain and chronic inflammation.

What to Expect
Physiological Changes: Many people experience ketosis, where the body uses fat for fuel instead of carbohydrates. Appetite regulation often improves, leading to natural calorie reduction without hunger.

Adaptation Period: It's normal to experience some adjustment symptoms (e.g., fatigue, headaches) as the body transitions to burning fat for energy.

Listening to your body is crucial. Some may find they need more fat or salt, while others thrive on leaner cuts of meat. Adapt the diet to suit your needs and goals.

Common Challenges and How to Overcome Them

Like any lifestyle change, the carnivore diet comes with its own set of challenges.

Initial Adaptation
Many experience symptoms of the "keto flu," including fatigue, brain fog, and muscle cramps, as the body adjusts to low carbohydrate intake.
Staying hydrated and ensuring adequate electrolyte intake (especially sodium) can ease these symptoms.

Digestive Changes
Switching to a meat-based diet may temporarily disrupt digestion. Eating fattier cuts of meat and incorporating bone broth can help.

Cravings
Cravings for sweets or carbs are common in the first few weeks. Focus on nutrient-dense meals, and don't be afraid to eat more meat to curb hunger.

Staying Motivated
Remind yourself of your goals and track your progress to stay committed. Celebrate small wins, whether it's improved energy, better sleep, or weight loss.

Social Situations
Navigating social events can be tricky. Plan ahead by eating before gatherings or bringing carnivore-friendly options like grilled meats or deviled eggs.

Meal Planning
Keep meals simple to avoid burnout. Focus on easy-to-prepare staples like steak, eggs, and bacon. Having a weekly meal plan can save time and reduce stress.

Most importantly, remember that this is a personal journey. Progress may look different for everyone, and setbacks are part of the process. The long-term benefits of improved health, mental clarity, and vitality are well worth the initial challenges.

You've already taken the first step by exploring the carnivore lifestyle. Let this chapter and the rest of this book be your guide, giving you the tools and confidence to embrace this transformative way of eating.

BREAKFAST

CARNIVORE BREAKFAST SAUSAGE PATTIES

Start your morning with these savory Carnivore Breakfast Sausage Patties. Made from fresh ground pork and a blend of simple seasonings, these patties are a satisfying way to fuel your day. Juicy, flavorful, and perfectly crisped, they're quick to prepare and ideal for the carnivore diet.

PREP TIME:
10 MINS

COOK TIME:
10 MINS

SERVING
4

INGREDIENTS

1 lb ground pork (preferably with some fat content)
1 tsp salt
1/2 tsp black pepper
1/2 tsp garlic powder
1/4 tsp smoked paprika

Note: *For a strict carnivore version, omit any garnishes shown in the images.*

INSTRUCTIONS

1. In a deep-bottom bowl, combine the ground pork, salt, crushed pepper, garlic powder, and smoked paprika. Mix thoroughly with your hands until the seasonings are evenly incorporated.
2. Divide the mixture into 8 segments and shape each into a flat, round patty about 1/2 inch thick.
3. Heat a cast-iron skillet over moderate flame. Once hot, add patties to the pan, spacing them apart for even cooking.
4. Cook the patties for 4–5 minutes on one side until the bottoms are golden brown and slightly crisp.
5. Flip the patties and cook for 4–5 minutes more.
6. Remove the patties and put them aside to rest for a minute before serving. Enjoy them hot as is, or pair them with fried eggs for a complete carnivore breakfast.

NUTRITION
CALORIES: 220, PROTEIN: 18G, CARBOHYDRATES: 0G, FAT: 16G

CARNIVORE OMELET WITH GROUND BEEF

This Carnivore Omelet with Ground Beef is a hearty, protein-packed breakfast option perfect for the carnivore diet. With just a handful of ingredients, it's simple to prepare yet incredibly satisfying.

PREP TIME:
5 MINS

COOK TIME:
10 MINS

SERVING
2

INGREDIENTS

4 large eggs
1/2 lb ground beef
2 tbsp butter
1/4 cup shredded cheese (optional)
1/2 tsp garlic powder
Salt and pepper to taste

Note: *For a strict carnivore version, omit any garnishes shown in the images.*

INSTRUCTIONS

1. Heat a skillet over moderate flame and add ground beef. Cook until browned and fully done, breaking it apart with a spatula. Season with garlic powder, salt, and pepper. Remove from the skillet and set aside.
2. Grab the shallow bowl and whisk the eggs until fully blended.
3. Use the same skillet, add butter, and allow it to melt over moderate flame. Ladle in the whisked eggs.
4. Leave the eggs to cook undisturbed for 1–2 minutes, then gently push the edges toward the center.
5. Once the eggs are mostly set, add cooked ground beef and cheese (if using) to one side of the omelet.
6. Fold the omelet in half, cook for more 1–2 minutes, and slide it onto a plate. Serve hot.

NUTRITION

CALORIES: 350, PROTEIN: 28G, CARBOHYDRATES: 1G, FAT: 26G

SMOKED SALMON AND SCRAMBLED EGGS

Enjoy the creamy goodness of scrambled eggs paired with the rich, smoky flavor of salmon. This Smoked Salmon and Scrambled Eggs dish is a luxurious way to start your day on the carnivore diet.

PREP TIME:
5 MINS

COOK TIME:
5 MINS

SERVING
2

INGREDIENTS

4 large eggs
3 oz smoked salmon, thinly sliced
2 tbsp butter
2 tbsp heavy cream (optional)
1/4 tsp dried dill (optional)
Salt and pepper to taste

INSTRUCTIONS

1. Crack the eggs into a bowl, add heavy cream (if using), and whisk until smooth. Season with salt (just a pinch) and pepper.
2. Heat butter in a skillet until melted. Drop the eggs into the skillet and allow them to cook undisturbed for 30 seconds.
3. Stir the eggs gently, folding them from the edges to the center, forming soft curds. Continue stirring until mostly set but still creamy.
4. Add smoked salmon to the skillet and gently fold it into the eggs. Cook for more than 30 seconds to warm through.
5. Sprinkle with dried dill (if using) and serve immediately.

Note: *For a strict carnivore version, omit any garnishes shown in the images.*

NUTRITION

CALORIES: 250, PROTEIN: 20G, CARBOHYDRATES: 1G, FAT: 20G

LAMB CHOP BREAKFAST PLATTER

Kickstart your day with this savory Lamb Chop Breakfast Platter. Juicy lamb chops paired with a pat of melted butter make for a rich and satisfying meal that's perfect for the carnivore diet.

PREP TIME:
5 MINS

COOK TIME:
10 MINS

SERVING
2

INGREDIENTS

4 small lamb chops (about 4 oz each)
2 tbsp butter
1 tsp garlic powder
1/2 tsp smoked paprika
Salt and pepper to taste

Note: *For a strict carnivore version, omit any garnishes shown in the images.*

INSTRUCTIONS

1. Pat the lamb chops dry and powder it on both sides with garlic powder, smoked paprika, salt, and crushed pepper.
2. Heat a cast-iron skillet over moderate flame and add one tbsp butter. Allow it to melt thoroughly, and coat the pan.
3. Place the lamb chops and sear for 3–4 minutes on one side.
4. Flip the chops and cook for more 3–4 minutes, basting with the leftover butter during the last minute of cooking.
5. Remove from the skillet and let the chops rest for 2 minutes before serving. Enjoy with additional melted butter if desired.

NUTRITION
CALORIES: 380, PROTEIN: 28G, CARBOHYDRATES: 0G, FAT: 30G,

BEEF FAT-FRIED CHICKEN THIGHS

Crispy on the outside, juicy on the inside—these Beef Fat-Fried Chicken Thighs are a carnivore's dream. Fried in rich beef tallow, they develop a golden crust while locking in moisture, making every bite deeply flavorful and satisfying. Perfect for a quick, high-fat, protein-packed meal!

PREP TIME:
5 MINS

COOK TIME:
15 MINS

SERVING
4

INGREDIENTS

1 lb. chicken thighs, skin-on
2 tbsp beef tallow
2 tbsp butter
2 egg yolks
1 tsp sea salt

INSTRUCTIONS

1. Heat a skillet on moderately high heat and add beef tallow.
2. Powder the chicken thighs with salt and place them upside down in the pan.
3. Cook for 10 minutes until the skin is crispy, then flip and cook for eight more minutes.
4. Grab the small shallow bowl and whisk egg yolks with melted butter.
5. Drizzle egg yolk butter over chicken thighs before serving.

Note: *For a strict carnivore version, omit any garnishes shown in the images.*

NUTRITION

CALORIES: 520 | PROTEIN: 38G, CARBOHYDRATES: 0G, FAT: 42G

BEEF TALLOW-FRIED EGGS

Elevate your breakfast with these Beef Tallow-Fried Eggs. Crispy edges and creamy yolks make this simple dish a delicious staple for anyone following the carnivore diet.

PREP TIME:
2 MINS

COOK TIME:
5 MINS

SERVING
2

INGREDIENTS

4 large eggs
2 tbsp beef tallow
1/2 tsp smoked paprika (optional)
Salt and pepper to taste

INSTRUCTIONS

1. Heat the beef tallow in a non-stick or cast-iron skillet over moderate flame until melted and hot.
2. Crack the eggs, drop them directly into the skillet, being sure to keep the yolks intact. Sprinkle the eggs with salt (just a pinch), pepper, and smoked paprika, if desired.
3. Cook the eggs for 2–3 minutes until mostly set. Decrease the stove heat to low, cover the skillet with a lid, and cook for more 1–2 minutes until the yolks reach your preferred consistency.
4. Remove the eggs carefully with a spatula and serve immediately, garnished with a drizzle of melted tallow if desired.

Note: *For a strict carnivore version, omit any garnishes shown in the images.*

NUTRITION

CALORIES: 200, PROTEIN: 14G, CARBOHYDRATES: 0G, FAT: 18G,

CREAMY SCRAMBLED EGGS

A classic carnivore breakfast, these Creamy Scrambled Eggs with Butter are quick and easy to prepare. They're rich, satisfying, and perfect for starting your day.

PREP TIME:
5 MINS

COOK TIME:
10 MINS

SERVING
2

INGREDIENTS

3 large eggs
2 tbsp butter
Salt and pepper to taste

INSTRUCTIONS

1. Crack the eggs into a bowl and whisk them until the yolks and whites are fully combined.
2. Heat the butter in a non-stick skillet over low to medium heat until melted and slightly foamy.
3. Pour the eggs into the skillet and let them sit undisturbed for a few seconds.
4. Gently stir the eggs with a spatula, folding and scraping from the edges to the center as they cook.
5. Remove from heat when the eggs are slightly undercooked, as they will continue to cook off the heat. Season with salt and pepper to taste and serve warm.

Note: *For a strict carnivore version, omit any garnishes shown in the images.*

NUTRITION

CALORIES: 250, PROTEIN: 18G, CARBOHYDRATES: 0G, FAT: 20G,

BUTTER-BASTED SALMON BITES

These Butter-Basted Salmon Bites are rich, flavorful, and incredibly simple. Seared in butter until golden and flaky, they deliver a satisfying balance of crispy edges and tender, juicy centers. A perfect high-protein, high-fat meal that's ready in minutes!

PREP TIME:
5 MINS

COOK TIME:
5 MINS

SERVING
2

INGREDIENTS

8 oz salmon fillet, cut into bite-sized pieces
2 tbsp butter
1 tsp sea salt
1/2 tsp black pepper

INSTRUCTIONS

1. Heat butter in a skillet over medium heat.
2. Add salmon bites, season with salt and pepper, and sear for 2-3 minutes per side.
3. Baste with melted butter while cooking to enhance flavor and crispiness.
4. Remove from heat and serve warm.

Note: *For a strict carnivore version, omit any garnishes shown in the images.*

NUTRITION

CALORIES: 380, PROTEIN: 40G, CARBOHYDRATES: 0G, FAT: 24G,

EASY SALMON PATTIES

These Easy Salmon Patties are quick to prepare, delicious, and packed with protein and healthy fats. Perfect for breakfast or a quick snack, they're a versatile carnivore-friendly option.

PREP TIME:
5 MINS

COOK TIME:
10 MINS

SERVING
2

INGREDIENTS

1 cup canned salmon (boneless, skinless, and drained)
1 large egg
2 tbsp pork rind crumbs (or almond flour if preferred)
1 tbsp butter (for frying)
Salt and pepper to taste

Note: *For a strict carnivore version, omit any garnishes shown in the images.*

INSTRUCTIONS

1. In a mixing bowl, combine the canned salmon, egg, pork rind crumbs, salt, and pepper. Mix well until the ingredients are fully incorporated.
2. Divide the mixture into 4 equal portions and shape each into a small patty.
3. Heat the butter in a skillet over medium heat until melted and slightly foamy.
4. Add the salmon patties to the skillet and cook for 3–4 minutes on each side, or until golden brown and crispy.
5. Remove from the skillet and let cool slightly before serving.
6. Serve warm as a hearty breakfast or pair with eggs for a complete meal.

NUTRITION

CALORIES: 250, PROTEIN: 22G, CARBOHYDRATES: 1G, FAT: 17G,

DUCK EGGS AND CRISPY BACON

Rich and flavorful, Duck Eggs and Crispy Bacon offer a decadent breakfast option for the carnivore diet. With creamy yolks and crispy bacon, this dish is a simple yet satisfying way to start your day.

PREP TIME:
5 MINS

COOK TIME:
10 MINS

SERVING
2

INGREDIENTS

4 duck eggs
8 slices of bacon
2 tbsp butter
1/2 tsp garlic powder
1/4 tsp smoked paprika (optional)
Salt and pepper to taste

Note: *For a strict carnivore version, omit any garnishes shown in the images.*

INSTRUCTIONS

1. Heat a skillet over moderate flame and add bacon slices. Cook for 4–5 minutes on one side until crispy. Remove and put it aside on a paper towel to drain excess grease.
2. Drain excess fat, leaving about 1 tbsp. Add one tbsp butter to the skillet.
3. Crack the duck eggs into the skillet, ensuring the yolks remain intact. Cook over moderate flame for 2–3 minutes until the whites are set, but the yolks are runny.
4. Sprinkle garlic powder and smoked paprika over the eggs while cooking.
5. Plate the eggs and crispy bacon together, adding the leftover butter to the eggs if desired. Serve hot.

NUTRITION

CALORIES: 400, PROTEIN: 25G, CARBOHYDRATES: 0G, FAT: 35G,

POACHED EGGS WITH BONE BROTH SAUCE

Poached Eggs with Bone Broth Sauce is a nutrient-rich breakfast that combines perfectly cooked eggs with a savory bone broth reduction. It's a comforting and nourishing option for the carnivore diet.

PREP TIME:
5 MINS

COOK TIME:
10 MINS

SERVING
2

INGREDIENTS

4 large eggs
1 cup bone broth
2 tbsp butter
1/2 tsp garlic powder
1/4 tsp smoked paprika
Salt and pepper to taste

Note: For a strict carnivore version, omit any garnishes shown in the images.

INSTRUCTIONS

1. Heat bone broth in a saucepan over moderate flame. Simmer until reduced by half, then whisk in the butter, garlic powder, and smoked paprika. Adjust seasoning with salt and pepper.
2. Get a pot of water to a gentle simmer. Crack each egg into a small bowl.
3. Stir the water to create a whirlpool, then softly slide each egg into the center. Poach for 3–4 minutes until the white part is set and the yolks remain runny.
4. Remove the eggs and spread them to drain water on a paper towel.
5. Plate the poached eggs and drizzle the bone broth sauce over the top. Serve immediately.

NUTRITION
CALORIES: 200, PROTEIN: 18G, CARBOHYDRATES: 0G, FAT: 15G,

EGG AND CREAM CHEESE PANCAKE

This Egg and Cream Cheese Pancake is a fluffy, protein-rich treat that's perfect for a carnivore breakfast. With just three ingredients, it's quick, easy, and satisfying.

PREP TIME:
5 MINS

COOK TIME:
5 MINS

SERVING
2

INGREDIENTS

4 large eggs
4 oz cream cheese, softened
1/2 tsp vanilla extract (optional)
1 tbsp butter
1/4 tsp smoked paprika (optional)
Salt to taste

Note: *For a strict carnivore version, omit any garnishes shown in the images.*

INSTRUCTIONS

1. In a powerful food blender, combine the eggs, cream cheese, vanilla extract (if using), and salt (just a pinch). Blend on full power until the texture turns smooth and frothy.
2. Heat a non-stick skillet over moderate flame and add a small amount of butter.
3. Ladle in the batter to form small pancakes, about 4 inches in diameter.
4. Cook for 2–3 minutes on one side until bubbles form and the edges are set. Flip carefully and cook for more 1–2 minutes.
5. Transfer to the serving plate (should be high edges) and serve hot with melted butter on top.

NUTRITION

CALORIES: 250, PROTEIN: 14G, CARBOHYDRATES: 1G, FAT: 20G,

BAKED EGGS IN BONE BROTH

Baked Eggs in Bone Broth is a comforting and nutrient-dense dish, perfect for breakfast or a light meal. The rich bone broth enhances the creamy baked eggs for a flavorful carnivore meal.

PREP TIME:
5 MINS

COOK TIME:
10 MINS

SERVING
2

INGREDIENTS

4 large eggs
1 cup bone broth
2 tbsp butter
1/4 tsp smoked paprika
1/4 cup shredded cheese (optional)
Salt and pepper to taste

INSTRUCTIONS

1. Preheat oven to 375°F (190°C). Grease two small ramekins with butter.
2. Pour 1/2 cup of bone broth into each ramekin. Crack two eggs into each ramekin, keeping the yolks intact.
3. Powder it with salt, crushed pepper, and smoked paprika. Sprinkle cheese on top if desired.
4. Place the ramekins in roasting dish and fill the dish with hot water, ladle halfway of the ramekins.
5. Bake for 8–10 minutes. Remove carefully, let cool slightly, and serve warm.

Note: *For a strict carnivore version, omit any garnishes shown in the images.*

NUTRITION

CALORIES: 220, PROTEIN: 18G, CARBOHYDRATES: 0G, FAT: 17G,

GRILLED SAUSAGE WITH FRIED DUCK EGG

Grilled Sausage with Fried Duck Egg is a hearty and flavorful dish, combining savory sausage with the rich taste of duck eggs. It's a simple yet satisfying carnivore meal.

PREP TIME:
5 MINS

COOK TIME:
10 MINS

SERVING
2

INGREDIENTS

4 sausages (your choice, uncooked)
2 duck eggs
1 tbsp butter
1/2 tsp garlic powder
1/4 tsp smoked paprika
Salt and pepper to taste

INSTRUCTIONS

1. Preheat a grill pan or outdoor grill. Grill the sausages for 8–10 minutes, and keep turning occasionally until fully cooked and charred on the outside.
2. Heat a skillet over moderate flame and add butter.
3. Crack the duck eggs into the skillet and cook for 2–3 minutes.
4. Powder the eggs with garlic powder, smoked paprika, salt, and pepper.
5. Plate the sausages and top with the fried duck eggs. Serve hot.

Note: *For a strict carnivore version, omit any garnishes shown in the images.*

NUTRITION

CALORIES: 450, PROTEIN: 25G, CARBOHYDRATES: 0G, FAT: 40G,

SEARED BEEF HEART WITH BUTTERED EGGS

This nutrient-dense Seared Beef Heart with Buttered Eggs is a hearty and flavorful carnivore meal. The tender beef heart pairs perfectly with creamy fried eggs for a satisfying dish.

PREP TIME:
5 MINS

COOK TIME:
15 MINS

SERVING
2

INGREDIENTS

1/2 lb beef heart, thinly sliced
4 large eggs
2 tbsp butter
1/2 tsp garlic powder
1/4 tsp smoked paprika
Salt and pepper to taste

Note: For a strict carnivore version, omit any garnishes shown in the images.

INSTRUCTIONS

1. Heat one tbsp butter in a skillet over moderate flame. Add beef heart slices and season with garlic powder, smoked paprika, salt, and pepper.
2. Sear the beef heart for 2–3 minutes on one side until browned and tender. Remove from the skillet and set aside.
3. Decrease the stove heat to medium and add leftover butter to the skillet.
4. Crack the eggs and fry for 2–3 minutes until the white parts are set but still runny.
5. Plate the seared beef heart and top with the fried eggs.
6. Drizzle any leftover butter from the skillet over the eggs and serve immediately.

NUTRITION

CALORIES: 350, PROTEIN: 30G, CARBOHYDRATES: 0G, FAT: 25G,

LUNCH

GRILLED RIBEYE WITH GARLIC BUTTER

Savor the rich flavors of a perfectly grilled ribeye steak topped with garlic butter. This dish is simple yet indulgent, making it an ideal lunch option for the carnivore diet.

PREP TIME: 5 MINS

COOK TIME: 10 MINS

SERVING 2

INGREDIENTS

2 ribeye steaks (6–8 oz each)
2 tbsp butter
1 clove garlic, mashed
1 tsp fresh parsley, chopped (optional)
Salt and pepper to taste

INSTRUCTIONS

1. Preheat grill to medium-high heat. Massage the ribeye steaks with salt and pepper on both sides.
2. Place the steaks on the grill and cook for 4–5 minutes on one side until your desired level of doneness is reached.
3. In a small saucepan over low heat, melt the butter and add mashed garlic. Stir until fragrant, about 1 minute.
4. Remove the steaks from the grill and let them rest for 5 minutes.
5. Drizzle the garlic butter over the steaks, spread fresh parsley on top, and serve hot.

Note: *For a strict carnivore version, omit any garnishes shown in the images.*

NUTRITION

CALORIES: 450, PROTEIN: 40G, CARBOHYDRATES: 0G, FAT: 35G,

PAN-SEARED SALMON WITH LEMON BUTTER

This Pan-Seared Salmon with Lemon Butter is a quick and flavorful lunch option that combines tender salmon with a zesty butter sauce. Perfectly carnivore-friendly, it's nutritious and delicious.

PREP TIME:
5 MINS

COOK TIME:
10 MINS

SERVING
2

INGREDIENTS

2 salmon fillets (6 oz each)
2 tbsp butter
1 tbsp fresh lemon juice
1/2 tsp garlic powder
Salt and pepper to taste

INSTRUCTIONS

1. Pat the fish fillets dry and powder them with salt, pepper, and garlic powder.
2. Heat a skillet over moderate flame and add one tbsp butter.
3. Place the salmon skin-side down in the skillet and sear for 4–5 minutes. Flip and cook for 2–3 minutes until cooked through.
4. In a small, deep-bottom bowl, melt the leftover butter and mix in the lemon juice.
5. Drizzle lemon butter sauce over the cooked salmon and serve immediately.

Note: *For a strict carnivore version, omit any garnishes shown in the images.*

NUTRITION

CALORIES: 380, PROTEIN: 35G, CARBOHYDRATES: 0G, FAT: 26G,

PORK CHOPS WITH CRISPY CRACKLINGS

These Pork Chops with Crispy Cracklings deliver a perfect balance of juicy meat and crispy, flavorful fat. It's a satisfying and easy-to-make lunch for those on the carnivore diet.

PREP TIME:
5 MINS

COOK TIME:
15 MINS

SERVING
2

INGREDIENTS

2 bone-in pork chops (6–8 oz each)
2 tbsp pork lard or tallow
1 tsp garlic powder
1/2 tsp smoked paprika
Salt and pepper to taste

Note: *For a strict carnivore version, omit any garnishes shown in the images.*

INSTRUCTIONS

1. Pat the pork chops dry and powder it with garlic powder, smoked paprika, salt, and crushed pepper.
2. Heat a cast-iron skillet over moderate flame and add pork lard or tallow.
3. Place the pork chops in the skillet and sear for 4–5 minutes on one side until golden brown and crispy.
4. Flip the chops and cook for more 4–5 minutes, reducing the heat if necessary.
5. Remove the chops and put them aside to rest for 5 minutes. Serve with the rendered crispy fat from the pan.

NUTRITION

CALORIES: 400, PROTEIN: 30G, CARBOHYDRATES: 0G, FAT: 30G,

LAMB SHANK STEW

This Lamb Shank Stew is a slow-cooked masterpiece of tender meat and rich broth, perfect for a hearty and nourishing lunch. The flavors deepen as they simmer, making every bite satisfying.

PREP TIME:
10 MINS

COOK TIME:
2 HOURS

SERVING
4

INGREDIENTS

2 lamb shanks (about 1.5 lbs total)
2 cups bone broth
2 tbsp butter
1 tsp garlic powder
1/2 tsp smoked paprika
Salt and pepper to taste

Note: *For a strict carnivore version, omit any garnishes shown in the images.*

INSTRUCTIONS

1. Heat a large pot over moderate flame and add butter. Brown the lamb shanks on all sides for about 5 minutes.
2. Remove the shanks and set aside. Deglaze the pot with 1/2 cup bone broth, scraping up any browned bits.
3. Return the lamb shanks and add leftover bone broth, garlic powder, smoked paprika, salt, and pepper.
4. Get it to a boil, then reduce to a low simmer. Cover and cook for two hours, turning the shanks occasionally.
5. Remove the lid and simmer for more 20 minutes to reduce the broth slightly. Serve hot with the broth poured over the lamb.

NUTRITION

CALORIES: 350, PROTEIN: 32G, CARBOHYDRATES: 0G, FAT: 25G,

SMOKED BRISKET WITH BONE BROTH GLAZE

Smoked Brisket with Bone Broth Glaze is a rich, slow-cooked dish that highlights the tender texture and smoky flavor of brisket, enhanced by a savory glaze. Perfect for a filling carnivore lunch.

PREP TIME:
15 MINS

COOK TIME:
6 HOURS

SERVING
6

INGREDIENTS

- 2 lbs beef brisket
- 2 cups bone broth
- 2 tbsp butter
- 1 tsp garlic powder
- 1/2 tsp smoked paprika
- Salt and pepper to taste

INSTRUCTIONS

1. Massage the brisket generously with garlic powder, smoked paprika, salt, and pepper.
2. Preheat smoker to 225°F (110°C). Place the brisket on the smoker and cook for 5–6 hours.
3. While smoking, heat the bone broth in a saucepan over moderate flame. Reduce by half, then whisk in the butter to create a glaze.
4. Once the brisket is done, brush the glaze over the meat and put it aside to rest for 15 minutes.
5. Slice the brisket, then drizzle with additional glaze, and serve.

Note: *For a strict carnivore version, omit any garnishes shown in the images.*

NUTRITION

CALORIES: 450, PROTEIN: 40G, CARBOHYDRATES: 0G, FAT: 35G,

ROASTED CHICKEN WINGS WITH BEEF FAT DRIZZLE

Crispy and flavorful, these Roasted Chicken Wings with Beef Fat Drizzle are a simple yet satisfying lunch option for the carnivore diet. The beef fat adds a rich, savory finish to the perfectly roasted wings.

PREP TIME:
5 MINS

COOK TIME:
40 MINS

SERVING
4

INGREDIENTS

2 lbs chicken wings
2 tbsp beef fat (tallow)
1 tsp garlic powder
1/2 tsp smoked paprika
Salt and pepper to taste

Note: *For a strict carnivore version, omit any garnishes shown in the images.*

INSTRUCTIONS

1. Preheat oven to 400°F (200°C). Arrange the baking sheet with parchment paper.
2. Pat the chicken wings dry and powder them with garlic powder, smoked paprika, salt, and crushed pepper.
3. Place the wings on the paper-arranged baking sheet in one layer (don't overlap) and roast for 35–40 minutes; flip after halftime has passed until golden brown and crispy.
4. In a small saucepan, melt the beef fat over low heat.
5. Once the wings are out of the oven, drizzle the melted beef fat over them and toss to coat evenly.
6. Serve immediately, garnished with an optional sprinkle of smoked paprika.

NUTRITION

CALORIES: 350, PROTEIN: 30G, CARBOHYDRATES: 0G, FAT: 25G,

BUTTER-POACHED DUCK LEGS

Indulge in the rich, tender perfection of Butter-Poached Duck Legs, where slow-poaching in butter transforms the meat into a melt-in-your-mouth delight. This simple yet luxurious dish delivers deep flavor and crispy skin, making it an ultimate carnivore-friendly meal.

PREP TIME:
5 MINS

COOK TIME:
10 MINS

SERVING
2

INGREDIENTS

2 duck legs
½ cup butter
3 cups bone broth
2 egg yolks
1 tsp sea salt

INSTRUCTIONS

1. In a deep pan, melt butter over low heat.
2. Add duck legs, powder them with salt, and cover them with bone broth.
3. Simmer on low heat for 2 hours until tender.
4. Remove duck legs and whisk egg yolks into the broth to create a rich sauce.
5. Pour the sauce over the duck and serve.

Note: *For a strict carnivore version, omit any garnishes shown in the images.*

NUTRITION
CALORIES: 720, PROTEIN: 45G, CARBOHYDRATES: 0G, FAT: 58G,

BONE BROTH-BRAISED LAMB RIBS

Rich and flavorful, this Crispy Duck Breast with Savory Sauce is a luxurious and satisfying lunch option for the carnivore diet. The crispy skin pairs beautifully with the simple yet delicious sauce.

PREP TIME:
5 MINS

COOK TIME:
20 MINS

SERVING
4

INGREDIENTS

1.5 lb. lamb ribs
4 cups beef bone broth
2 tbsp butter
1 tbsp beef tallow
1 tsp sea salt

INSTRUCTIONS

1. In a large shallow pot, sear lamb ribs in beef tallow for 5 minutes on one side.
2. Pour in bone broth and get it to a boil. Decrease the stove heat and simmer for 3 hours until tender.
3. Remove the ribs and mix in butter with the broth to create a glaze. Pour the glaze over the ribs and serve.

Note: *For a strict carnivore version, omit any garnishes shown in the images.*

NUTRITION

CALORIES: 680 PROTEIN: 50G, CARBOHYDRATES: 0G, FAT: 52G,

GRILLED SAUSAGE AND BUTTER DIP

Simple yet indulgent, Grilled Sausage and Butter Dip combines juicy sausages with a rich, flavorful butter dip for a quick and satisfying carnivore-friendly lunch.

PREP TIME:
5 MINS

COOK TIME:
10 MINS

SERVING
2

INGREDIENTS

4 sausages (uncooked, your choice)
2 tbsp butter
1/2 tsp garlic powder
1/4 tsp smoked paprika
Salt and pepper to taste

Note: *For a strict carnivore version, omit any garnishes shown in the images.*

INSTRUCTIONS

1. Preheat a grill or grill pan. Grill the sausages for 8–10 minutes, and keep turning occasionally until fully cooked and charred on the outside.
2. In a small saucepan over low heat, melt the butter and toss in the garlic powder and smoked paprika. Powder it with salt and crushed pepper to taste.
3. Arrange the grilled sausages on a plate and serve with the butter dip on the side for dipping.
4. Optionally drizzle some of the butter dips over the sausages before serving.

NUTRITION
CALORIES: 450, PROTEIN: 25G, CARBOHYDRATES: 0G, FAT: 40G,

BEEF TENDERLOIN AND BONE MARROW PLATE

This Beef Tenderloin and Bone Marrow Plate is a rich and elegant carnivore-friendly meal. The tender beef pairs perfectly with the buttery, nutrient-dense bone marrow for a satisfying lunch.

PREP TIME: 10 MINS

COOK TIME: 20 MINS

SERVING 2

INGREDIENTS

2 beef tenderloin steaks (6 oz each)
2 bone marrow pieces (cut lengthwise)
2 tbsp butter
1/2 tsp garlic powder
1/4 tsp smoked paprika
Salt and pepper to taste

Note: *For a strict carnivore version, omit any garnishes shown in the images.*

INSTRUCTIONS

1. Preheat oven to 425°F (220°C). Place the bone marrow pieces on the parchment paper-arranged baking sheet, powder it with salt, and roast for 15–20 minutes until soft and bubbling.
2. While the marrow roasts, massage the beef tenderloin steaks with garlic powder, smoked paprika, salt, and pepper.
3. Heat a skillet over moderate flame and add butter. Sear the steaks for 3–4 minutes on one side for medium-rare, or adjust the time for desired doneness.
4. Remove the steaks and put them aside to rest for 5 minutes.
5. Serve the tenderloin steaks alongside the roasted bone marrow, spooning the marrow over the beef if desired.

NUTRITION

CALORIES: 500, PROTEIN: 40G, CARBOHYDRATES: 0G, FAT: 40G,

PAN-FRIED PORK CUTLETS WITH DUCK FAT

Enjoy these tender and flavorful Pan-Fried Pork Cutlets cooked in rich duck fat. This quick and simple carnivore-friendly dish is perfect for lunch, delivering a satisfying blend of juicy meat and crispy edges.

PREP TIME: 5 MINS

COOK TIME: 10 MINS

SERVING 2

INGREDIENTS

4 pork cutlets (about 4 oz each)
2 tbsp duck fat
1/2 tsp garlic powder
1/2 tsp smoked paprika
Salt and pepper to taste

Note: *For a strict carnivore version, omit any garnishes shown in the images.*

INSTRUCTIONS

1. Pat the pork cutlets dry and powder them with garlic powder, smoked paprika, salt, and
2. crushed pepper.
3. Heat the duck fat over a moderate flame until hot.
4. Place the cutlets in the skillet and cook for 3–4 minutes on one side until golden brown and crispy.
5. Flip the cutlets and cook for more 3–4 minutes, adjusting the heat as needed to prevent burning.
6. Remove the pork cutlets from the skillet and let them rest for 2 minutes before serving.
7. Drizzle any leftover duck fat over the cutlets for extra flavor.

NUTRITION

CALORIES: 350, PROTEIN: 30G, CARBOHYDRATES: 0G, FAT: 25G,

CRAB MEAT WITH GARLIC BUTTER SAUCE

Tender crab meat paired with a rich garlic butter sauce makes for a luxurious and flavorful lunch. This simple dish is light yet satisfying, perfect for the carnivore diet.

PREP TIME: 5 MINS

COOK TIME: 10 MINS

SERVING 2

INGREDIENTS

1/2 lb lump crab meat
2 tbsp butter
1 clove garlic, mashed
1 tbsp lemon juice (optional)
Salt and pepper to taste

INSTRUCTIONS

1. Heat two tbsp butter in a skillet over moderate flame. Add mashed garlic and sauté for 1–2 minutes until fragrant.
2. Add crab meat to the skillet and gently stir to coat it with garlic butter.
3. Cook for 3–4 minutes, being careful not to break the crab meat apart.
4. Add lemon juice, if using, and powder it with salt and pepper to taste.
5. Serve immediately, drizzled with the garlic butter sauce.

Note: *For a strict carnivore version, omit any garnishes shown in the images.*

NUTRITION

CALORIES: 200, PROTEIN: 20G, CARBOHYDRATES: 0G, FAT: 15G,

LAMB RIBS WITH HERB-INFUSED BUTTER

Juicy and flavorful, these Lamb Ribs with Herb-Infused Butter are a delicious and hearty lunch option. The buttery herb glaze enhances the rich flavor of the tender ribs.

PREP TIME: 10 MINS

COOK TIME: 45 MINS

SERVING 4

INGREDIENTS

2 lbs lamb ribs
2 tbsp butter
1 tsp garlic powder
1 tsp fresh rosemary, chopped (optional)
Salt and pepper to taste

INSTRUCTIONS

1. Preheat oven to 375°F (190°C). Massage the lamb ribs with garlic powder, salt, and pepper.
2. Place the ribs on the parchment paper-arranged baking sheet and roast for 40 minutes; flip after halftime has passed.
3. In a small saucepan, melt the butter over low heat and toss in the chopped rosemary.
4. Remove the lamb ribs and brush with the herb-infused butter.
5. Return the ribs to the oven for more 5 minutes to absorb the flavors.
6. Serve hot, drizzled with any leftover butter.

Note: *For a strict carnivore version, omit any garnishes shown in the images.*

NUTRITION

CALORIES: 450, PROTEIN: 35G, CARBOHYDRATES: 0G, FAT: 35G,

CRISPY DUCK WINGS WITH TALLOW DIP

Golden, crispy, and packed with flavor, these Crispy Duck Wings are roasted to perfection and paired with a rich tallow dip for extra indulgence. With a crunchy skin and tender meat, they make the perfect high-fat, protein-packed carnivore treat!

PREP TIME: 10 MINS

COOK TIME: 10 MINS

SERVING 4

INGREDIENTS

1.5 lbs duck wings
3 tbsp beef tallow
1 tsp sea salt
1/2 tsp black pepper

INSTRUCTIONS

1. Preheat oven to 400°F (200°C).
2. Toss duck wings with 2 tbsp melted beef tallow, salt, and crushed pepper.
3. Arrange wings on the parchment-paper-arranged baking sheet and roast for 40-45 minutes, flipping after halftime has passed.
4. Heat the leftover one tbsp beef tallow and serve it like dipping sauce with the crispy wings.

Note: *For a strict carnivore version, omit any garnishes shown in the images.*

NUTRITION
CALORIES: 400, PROTEIN: 30G, CARBOHYDRATES: 0G, FAT: 30G,

SEARED COD WITH BEEF FAT SAUCE

Delicate and flaky, Seared Cod with Beef Fat Sauce is a light yet flavorful carnivore-friendly lunch. The beef fat enhances the cod's natural flavor, making it a rich and satisfying dish.

PREP TIME: 5 MINS

COOK TIME: 10 MINS

SERVING 2

INGREDIENTS

2 cod fillets (6 oz each)
2 tbsp beef fat (tallow)
1/2 tsp garlic powder
1/4 tsp smoked paprika
Salt and pepper to taste

INSTRUCTIONS

1. Pat the cod fillets dry and massage with garlic powder, smoked paprika, salt, and pepper.
2. Heat the beef fat over moderate flame until hot.
3. Place the cod fillets in the skillet and sear for 3–4 minutes on one side.
4. Flip the fillets and cook for more 2–3 minutes until the fillet flakes easily.
5. Drizzle any leftover beef fat from the skillet over the fillets before serving.

Note: *For a strict carnivore version, omit any garnishes shown in the images.*

NUTRITION

CALORIES: 300, PROTEIN: 30G, CARBOHYDRATES: 0G, FAT: 20G,

DINNER

SLOW-COOKED BEEF SHORT RIBS

Savor the rich flavors of a perfectly grilled ribeye steak topped with garlic butter. This dish is simple yet indulgent, making it an ideal lunch option for the carnivore diet.

PREP TIME: 10 MINS

COOK TIME: 4-6 HOURS

SERVING 4

INGREDIENTS

2 lbs beef short ribs
2 cups bone broth
2 tbsp butter
1 tsp garlic powder
1/2 tsp smoked paprika
Salt and pepper to taste

Note: *For a strict carnivore version, omit any garnishes shown in the images.*

INSTRUCTIONS

1. Massage the beef short ribs with garlic powder, smoked paprika, salt, and pepper.
2. Heat a large skillet over moderate flame and sear the ribs on all sides. Remove and set aside.
3. In a slow cooker, add bone broth and butter. Place the seared short ribs in the slow cooker.
4. Cover and cook on low flame for 6 hours or on high for 4 hours.
5. Remove the ribs and reduce the cooking liquid in a saucepan if desired for a thicker sauce.
6. Serve the ribs with a drizzle of sauce over the top.

NUTRITION

CALORIES: 450, PROTEIN: 35G, CARBOHYDRATES: 0G, FAT: 35G,

ROAST LEG OF LAMB WITH PAN JUICES

A classic and elegant dish, this Roast Leg of Lamb with Pan Juices is perfect for a satisfying carnivore dinner. The natural juices enhance the lamb's rich flavor for a succulent meal.

PREP TIME: 15 MINS

COOK TIME: 1-2 HOURS

SERVING: 6

INGREDIENTS

4 lbs leg of lamb (bone-in)
3 tbsp butter
1 tsp garlic powder
1 tsp fresh rosemary, chopped (optional)
Salt and pepper to taste

Note: *For a strict carnivore version, omit any garnishes shown in the images.*

INSTRUCTIONS

1. Preheat oven to 375°F (190°C). Massage the lamb generously with garlic powder, rosemary, salt, and pepper.
2. Place the lamb in a roasting pan and dot with butter.
3. Roast the lamb for 90–120 minutes, basting occasionally with the pan juices, until the food thermometer shows internal temperature readings of 135°F (medium-rare) or your preferred doneness.
4. Remove the lamb from the oven and put it aside to rest for 15 minutes.
5. Slice and serve with the pan juices.

NUTRITION

CALORIES: 450, PROTEIN: 38G, CARBOHYDRATES: 0G, FAT: 33G,

PORK LOIN WITH BUTTER HERB GLAZE

Juicy and tender, this Pork Loin with Butter Herb Glaze is a flavorful and satisfying dish perfect for dinner. The herb-infused butter elevates the natural flavors of the pork.

PREP TIME: 10 MINS

COOK TIME: 1 HOUR

SERVING 4

INGREDIENTS

2 lbs pork loin
3 tbsp butter
1 tsp garlic powder
1 tsp dried thyme or rosemary
Salt and pepper to taste

INSTRUCTIONS

1. Preheat oven to 375°F (190°C). Massage the pork loin with garlic powder, thyme, salt, and pepper.
2. Heat a skillet over moderate flame and sear the pork loin on all sides.
3. Transfer the pork to a roasting pan. Spread 2 tbsp of butter over the top.
4. Roast for 50–60 minutes until the food thermometer shows internal temperature readings of 145°F.
5. In a small saucepan, melt the leftover butter and mix with the pan drippings. Drizzle the glaze over the sliced pork before serving.

Note: *For a strict carnivore version, omit any garnishes shown in the images.*

NUTRITION

CALORIES: 380, PROTEIN: 40G, CARBOHYDRATES: 0G, FAT: 25G,

GRILLED SALMON WITH CRISPY SKIN

Perfectly Grilled Salmon with Crispy Skin is a light yet indulgent dinner option. The crispy skin adds texture and flavor, making this dish a carnivore favorite.

PREP TIME: 5 MINS

COOK TIME: 10 MINS

SERVING 2

INGREDIENTS

2 salmon fillets (6 oz each)
2 tbsp butter
1 tsp garlic powder
1/2 tsp smoked paprika
Salt and pepper to taste

Note: *For a strict carnivore version, omit any garnishes shown in the images.*

INSTRUCTIONS

1. Pat the salmon fillets dry and massage the skin side with salt and the flesh side with garlic powder, smoked paprika, and pepper.
2. Heat a skillet over moderate flame and add one tbsp butter.
3. Place the fish fillets skin-side down and cook for 4–5 minutes. Don't touch this time to achieve crispy skin.
4. Flip the fillets and cook for more 2–3 minutes, adding the leftover butter.
5. Serve the salmon with a drizzle of melted butter from the skillet.

NUTRITION

CALORIES: 380, PROTEIN: 35G, CARBOHYDRATES: 0G, FAT: 26G,

WHOLE ROASTED CHICKEN WITH TALLOW RUB

This Whole Roasted Chicken with Tallow Rub is a flavorful and juicy dinner option. The beef tallow adds richness and keeps the chicken tender while roasting.

PREP TIME: 10 MINS

COOK TIME: 1.5 HOURS

SERVING: 4

INGREDIENTS

1 whole chicken (4–5 lbs)
3 tbsp beef tallow
1 tsp garlic powder
1 tsp smoked paprika
Salt and pepper to taste

Note: *For a strict carnivore version, omit any garnishes shown in the images.*

INSTRUCTIONS

1. Preheat oven to 400°F (200°C). Pat the chicken dry and massage with garlic powder, smoked paprika, salt, and pepper.
2. Rub the beef tallow all over the chicken, including under the skin, if possible.
3. Place the chicken in a roasting pan and roast for 90 minutes until the food thermometer shows a reading of internal in the thickest part of the thigh reaches 165°F.
4. Baste the chicken with the rendered fat halfway through cooking for extra flavor.
5. Put the chicken to rest for 10 minutes before carving. Serve with the pan drippings as a sauce.

NUTRITION

CALORIES: 400, PROTEIN: 35G, CARBOHYDRATES: 0G, FAT: 28G,

DUCK CONFIT WITH CRISPY SKIN

Duck Confit with Crispy Skin is a luxurious dish that's rich, flavorful, and perfect for a carnivore dinner. The slow-cooked duck is tender on the inside, while the skin is golden and crispy.

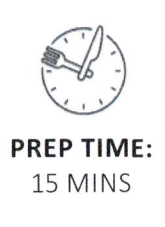

PREP TIME: 15 MINS

COOK TIME: 2 HOURS

SERVING 2

INGREDIENTS

2 duck legs (bone-in)
1 cup duck fat
1 tsp garlic powder
1 tsp fresh thyme leaves (optional)
Salt and pepper to taste

INSTRUCTIONS

1. Preheat oven to 300°F (150°C). Pat the duck legs dry and season with garlic powder, thyme, salt, and pepper.
2. Place the duck legs in an oven dish and cover with melted duck fat.
3. Bake for 120 minutes until the meat is tender.
4. Remove the legs and place them skin-side down in a hot skillet over moderate flame. Cook for 3–4 minutes until the skin looks crispy.
5. Serve the duck legs hot, optionally drizzled with a small amount of the reserved duck fat.

Note: *For a strict carnivore version, omit any garnishes shown in the images.*

NUTRITION

CALORIES: 500, PROTEIN: 25G, CARBOHYDRATES: 0G, FAT: 45G,

PAN-SEARED SCALLOPS WITH BUTTER

These pan-seared scallops with butter are a quick and elegant dish. The golden crust and rich buttery flavor make this a perfect choice for a light and satisfying carnivore dinner.

PREP TIME: 5 MINS

COOK TIME: 5 MINS

SERVING 2

INGREDIENTS

8 large scallops
2 tbsp butter
1/2 tsp garlic powder
1 tsp lemon juice (optional)
Salt and pepper to taste

INSTRUCTIONS

1. Pat the scallops dry and powder them with garlic powder, salt, and pepper.
2. Heat a skillet over moderate flame and add one tbsp butter.
3. Place the scallops in the skillet and sear for 2 minutes on one side without moving them.
4. Flip the scallops and cook for more 1–2 minutes until golden and cooked through.
5. Add leftover butter and optional lemon juice to the skillet, spooning it over the scallops before serving.

Note: *For a strict carnivore version, omit any garnishes shown in the images.*

NUTRITION

CALORIES: 220, PROTEIN: 25G, CARBOHYDRATES: 0G, FAT: 12G,

GRILLED SWORDFISH WITH BONE MARROW BUTTER

Grilled Swordfish with Bone Marrow Butter is a rich and flavorful dish that combines the meaty texture of swordfish with the luxurious taste of bone marrow. A perfect carnivore-friendly dinner.

PREP TIME: 10 MINS

COOK TIME: 10 MINS

SERVING 2

INGREDIENTS

2 swordfish steaks (6 oz each)
2 tbsp bone marrow (melted)
1 tsp garlic powder
1/2 tsp smoked paprika
Salt and pepper to taste

INSTRUCTIONS

1. Preheat grill to medium-high heat. Massage the swordfish steaks with garlic powder, smoked paprika, salt, and pepper.
2. Grill the swordfish for 4–5 minutes on one side until cooked through.
3. While the fish is grilling, melt the bone marrow in a small saucepan over low heat.
4. Drizzle the melted bone marrow butter over the grilled swordfish before serving.
5. Serve hot with additional melted marrow on the side if desired.

Note: *For a strict carnivore version, omit any garnishes shown in the images.*

NUTRITION

CALORIES: 350, PROTEIN: 35G, CARBOHYDRATES: 0G, FAT: 20G,

SLOW-ROASTED LAMB SHOULDER

Tender, juicy, and bursting with rich flavor, this Slow-Roasted Lamb Shoulder is cooked low and slow until fall-apart delicious. Finished with a warm butter drizzle, it's a simple yet indulgent carnivore meal that satisfies every bite!

PREP TIME: 5 MINS

COOK TIME: 10 MINS

SERVING 2

INGREDIENTS

- 2 lbs lamb shoulder
- 4 tbsp butter
- 1 tsp sea salt
- 1/2 tsp black pepper

INSTRUCTIONS

1. Preheat oven to 300°F (150°C).
2. Season lamb shoulder with salt and pepper.
3. Place in a roasting dish and roast for 2.5 hours, basting occasionally.
4. Melt butter and drizzle over the lamb for the last 30 minutes of roasting.
5. Put it aside to rest for 10 minutes. Then slice and serve.

Note: *For a strict carnivore version, omit any garnishes shown in the images.*

NUTRITION
CALORIES: 670, PROTEIN: 50G, CARBOHYDRATES: 0G, FAT: 54G,

VENISON ROAST WITH GARLIC BUTTER SAUCE

This Venison Roast with Garlic Butter Sauce is tender, flavorful, and perfect for a hearty carnivore dinner. The garlic butter enhances the rich taste of the venison, making it a standout dish.

PREP TIME: 10 MINS

COOK TIME: 1 HOUR

SERVING 4

INGREDIENTS

2 lbs venison roast
3 tbsp butter
1 tsp garlic powder
1 tsp fresh thyme leaves (optional)
Salt and pepper to taste

INSTRUCTIONS

1. Preheat oven to 375°F (190°C). Massage the venison roast with garlic powder, thyme, salt, and pepper.
2. Heat one tbsp butter in an oven-safe skillet over moderate flame. Sear the meat until browned on all sides.
3. Transfer the skillet and roast for 46–50 minutes until the food thermometer shows internal temperature readings of 135°F (medium-rare).
4. Remove the venison from the skillet and let rest for 10 minutes.
5. Use the same skillet, melt the leftover butter over low heat. Drizzle the garlic butter sauce over the sliced venison and serve.

Note: *For a strict carnivore version, omit any garnishes shown in the images.*

NUTRITION

CALORIES: 350, PROTEIN: 35G, CARBOHYDRATES: 0G, FAT: 25G,

LAMB MEATBALLS IN BONE BROTH SAUCE

Tender and flavorful, these Lamb Meatballs in Bone Broth Sauce are a hearty and satisfying carnivore dish. The bone broth adds a rich depth of flavor, making this a comforting and nourishing dinner option.

PREP TIME: 10 MINS

COOK TIME: 20 MINS

SERVING 4

INGREDIENTS

1 lb ground lamb
1 egg
1 tsp garlic powder
2 cups bone broth
2 tbsp butter
Salt and pepper to taste

Note: *For a strict carnivore version, omit any garnishes shown in the images.*

INSTRUCTIONS

1. Grab the shallow bowl and combine the ground lamb, egg, garlic powder, salt, and pepper. Mix well and form into small 1 inch in diameter meatballs.
2. Heat one tbsp butter in a skillet over moderate flame. Brown the meatballs on all sides for about 5–6 minutes, then remove and set aside.
3. Use the same skillet, add bone broth and leftover butter. Get it to a simmer and scrape up any browned bits from the pan.
4. Return the meatballs to the skillet and simmer for 10 minutes, allowing the broth to reduce slightly.
5. Serve the meatballs hot, drizzled with the rich bone broth sauce.

NUTRITION

CALORIES: 300, PROTEIN: 25G, CARBOHYDRATES: 0G, FAT: 22G,

PORK BELLY ROAST WITH CRACKLING CRUST

Crispy on the outside and tender on the inside, this Pork Belly Roast with Crackling Crust is a show-stopping carnivore dish that's both indulgent and delicious.

PREP TIME: 10 MINS

COOK TIME: 1.5 HOURS

SERVING 4

INGREDIENTS

2 lbs pork belly
1 tsp garlic powder
1 tsp smoked paprika
2 tbsp beef fat (tallow)
Salt and pepper to taste

INSTRUCTIONS

1. Preheat oven to 425°F (220°C). Cut the skin of the pork belly in a crosshatch pattern, carfuly do it.
2. Rub the pork belly with garlic powder, smoked paprika, salt, and pepper.
3. Place the pork belly and roast for 20 minutes at 425°F to create a crispy crust.
4. Turn the oven heat leavel down to 325°F (165°C) and continue roasting for more hour until tender.
5. Put the pork belly aside to rest for 10 minutes before slicing. Serve with the crispy crackling on top.

Note: *For a strict carnivore version, omit any garnishes shown in the images.*

NUTRITION

CALORIES: 450, PROTEIN: 30G, CARBOHYDRATES: 0G, FAT: 35G,

GRILLED LOBSTER WITH BUTTER DIPPING SAUCE

Grilled Lobster with Butter Dipping Sauce is a luxurious and flavorful dinner option. The tender lobster meat pairs beautifully with the rich, buttery dipping sauce, making it a true carnivore delight.

PREP TIME: 10 MINS

COOK TIME: 10 MINS

SERVING 2

INGREDIENTS

2 lobster tails (6 oz each)
4 tbsp butter
1 tsp garlic powder
1 tsp lemon juice (optional)
Salt and pepper to taste

INSTRUCTIONS

1. Preheat grill to medium-high heat. Cut the lobster tails in half lengthwise and powder it with garlic powder, salt, and crushed pepper.
2. Place the lobster tails flesh-side down and grill for 4 minutes. Flip and cook more for 3–4 minutes until the meat is opaque and fully cooked.
3. In a small saucepan, melt the butter and mix in the garlic powder and lemon juice (if using).
4. Serve the grilled lobster tails hot with the butter dipping sauce on the side.

Note: *For a strict carnivore version, omit any garnishes shown in the images.*

NUTRITION

CALORIES: 300, PROTEIN: 25G, CARBOHYDRATES: 0G, FAT: 20G,

BRAISED OXTAIL IN BEEF STOCK

Rich and tender, Braised Oxtail in Beef Stock is a comforting carnivore dish that's perfect for dinner. The slow cooking process brings out deep, flavorful goodness in the oxtail.

PREP TIME: 15 MINS

COOK TIME: 3 HOURS

SERVING 4

INGREDIENTS

2 lbs oxtail
3 cups beef stock
2 tbsp butter
1 tsp garlic powder
1/2 tsp smoked paprika
Salt and pepper to taste

INSTRUCTIONS

1. Heat one tbsp butter in a deep-bottom pot over moderate flame. Brown the oxtail pieces on all sides, then remove and set aside.
2. Add beef stock to the pot, scraping up any browned bits. Toss in garlic powder, smoked paprika, salt, and pepper.
3. Return the oxtail to the pot, get it to a boil, then reduce to a simmer. Cover and cook for 2.5–3 hours until tender and falling off the bone.
4. Remove the oxtail from the pot and skim any excess fat from the cooking liquid.
5. Serve the oxtail hot with the reduced broth drizzled over the top.

Note: *For a strict carnivore version, omit any garnishes shown in the images.*

NUTRITION

CALORIES: 450, PROTEIN: 35G, CARBOHYDRATES: 0G, FAT: 35G,

FILET MIGNON WITH DUCK FAT GRAVY

This Filet Mignon with Duck Fat Gravy is an elegant carnivore dish. The tender filet mignon is enhanced by the rich, velvety duck fat gravy, making it a dinner to remember.

PREP TIME: 10 MINS

COOK TIME: 10 MINS

SERVING 2

INGREDIENTS

2 filet mignon steaks (6 oz each)
2 tbsp duck fat
1/2 cup bone broth
1 tsp garlic powder
Salt and pepper to taste

INSTRUCTIONS

1. Pat the filet mignon dry with paper towels and massage with garlic powder, salt, and crushed pepper.
2. Heat one tbsp duck fat in a skillet over moderate flame. Sear the steaks for 3–4 minutes on one side for medium-rare or adjust for desired doneness. Remove the steaks and let them rest.
3. Use the same skillet, add bone broth and leftover duck fat. Simmer for 2–3 minutes, scraping up any browned bits, until slightly reduced.
4. Spoon the duck fat gravy over the filet mignon and serve hot.

Note: *For a strict carnivore version, omit any garnishes shown in the images.*

NUTRITION

CALORIES: 400, PROTEIN: 35G, CARBOHYDRATES: 0G, FAT: 30G,

SNACKS & SMALL BITES

CHEWY PORK RIND BITES

These Chewy Pork Rind Bites deliver the perfect balance of crispy edges and a soft, chewy center. Slow-cooked and fried in tallow, they offer a deeply satisfying bite.

PREP TIME: 5 MINS

COOK TIME: 20 MINS

SERVING 4

INGREDIENTS

8 oz pork skin (cut into bite-sized pieces)
3 tbsp beef tallow
1 tsp sea salt
1/2 tsp black pepper

INSTRUCTIONS

1. Heat beef tallow in a skillet over medium heat.
2. Add pork skin pieces and cook for 10-12 minutes, stirring occasionally.
3. Increase heat to high and fry for another 5 minutes until crispy.
4. Remove from heat, season with salt and pepper, and enjoy warm.

Note: *For a strict carnivore version, omit any garnishes shown in the images.*

NUTRITION

CALORIES: 380, PROTEIN: 25G, CARBOHYDRATES: 0G, FAT: 32G,

BACON-WRAPPED CHEESE STICKS

These Bacon-Wrapped Cheese Sticks are a rich and flavorful snack that's quick to prepare. The crispy bacon complements the melted cheese for a carnivore-friendly treat.

PREP TIME: 5 MINS

COOK TIME: 10 MINS

SERVING 2

INGREDIENTS

4 cheese sticks (your choice, like mozzarella)
8 slices of bacon
1/2 tsp garlic powder
1/4 tsp smoked paprika
Salt and pepper to taste

INSTRUCTIONS

1. Preheat oven to 400°F (200°C). Arrange the baking sheet with parchment paper.
2. Wrap each cheese stick tightly with two slices of bacon, overlapping slightly.
3. Place the wrapped cheese sticks on the parchment paper-arranged baking sheet and season with garlic powder and smoked paprika.
4. Bake for 10 minutes until the bacon turns crispy.
5. Cool slightly before serving.

Note: *For a strict carnivore version, omit any garnishes shown in the images.*

NUTRITION

CALORIES: 350, PROTEIN: 25G, CARBOHYDRATES: 1G, FAT: 28G,

HARD-BOILED EGGS WITH SALTED BUTTER

Simple and satisfying, Hard-Boiled Eggs with Salted Butter is a quick snack that's perfect for the carnivore diet. The rich butter enhances the creamy eggs, making this a delicious option.

PREP TIME: 5 MINS

COOK TIME: 10 MINS

SERVING 2

INGREDIENTS

4 large eggs
2 tbsp salted butter
1/2 tsp smoked paprika (optional)
Salt and pepper to taste

INSTRUCTIONS

1. Place the eggs in a deep-bottom pot and cover with water. Get it to a boil, then decrease the stove heat and cook for 8–10 minutes.
2. Drain the hot water and shift the eggs to an ice bath. Let cool for 5 minutes, then peel. Slice the eggs in half and place on a serving plate.
3. Melt the butter in a small saucepan and drizzle it over the eggs. Sprinkle with smoked paprika if desired.
4. Serve immediately.

Note: *For a strict carnivore version, omit any garnishes shown in the images.*

NUTRITION

CALORIES: 200, PROTEIN: 12G, CARBOHYDRATES: 0G, FAT: 18G,

CARNIVORE EGG MUFFINS

Carnivore Egg Muffins are a protein-packed snack or mini-meal. Filled with eggs, crispy bacon, and melted cheese, these muffins are satisfying and easy to make.

PREP TIME: 5 MINS

COOK TIME: 20 MINS

SERVING 4

INGREDIENTS

6 large eggs
4 slices of bacon, cooked and crumbled
1/2 cup shredded cheese
1/2 tsp garlic powder
Salt and pepper to taste

Note: *For a strict carnivore version, omit any garnishes shown in the images.*

INSTRUCTIONS

1. Preheat oven to 375°F (190°C). Grease a muffin tin.
2. Whisk the eggs in a deep-bottom bowl and season with garlic powder, salt, and pepper.
3. Divide the crumbled bacon and shredded cheese evenly among the muffin cups.
4. Ladle the whisked eggs into each cup, filling them about 3/4 full.
5. Bake for 17–20 minutes until the muffins are set and golden on top.
6. Cool slightly before removing. Serve warm or store for later.

NUTRITION

CALORIES: 250, PROTEIN: 20G, CARBOHYDRATES: 1G, FAT: 20G,

LAMB MEATBALLS WITH BEEF FAT DRIZZLE

Juicy and flavorful Lamb Meatballs with Beef Fat Drizzle are a rich and savory snack. The beef fat adds a luxurious touch, making these meatballs irresistible.

PREP TIME: 10 MINS

COOK TIME: 15 MINS

SERVING 4

INGREDIENTS

1 lb ground lamb
1 egg
1/2 tsp garlic powder
2 tbsp beef fat (tallow)
Salt and pepper to taste

INSTRUCTIONS

1. Grab the shallow bowl and combine the ground lamb, egg, garlic powder, salt, and pepper. Mix well and form into small meatballs.
2. Heat one tbsp beef fat in a skillet over moderate flame. Add meatballs and cook for 10–12 minutes, turning occasionally, until browned and cooked through.
3. Remove the meatballs and drizzle with the leftover melted beef fat.
4. Serve hot, optionally garnished with a sprinkle of salt.

Note: *For a strict carnivore version, omit any garnishes shown in the images.*

NUTRITION

CALORIES: 300, PROTEIN: 22G, CARBOHYDRATES: 0G, FAT: 24G,

SMOKED SALMON ROLLS WITH CREAM CHEESE

Rich and creamy, these Smoked Salmon Rolls with Cream Cheese are a perfect carnivore-friendly snack. They are easy to prepare, making them ideal for a quick bite or appetizer.

PREP TIME: 10 MINS

COOK TIME: 00 MINS

SERVING 2

INGREDIENTS

4 oz smoked salmon
2 oz cream cheese, softened
1/2 tsp garlic powder
1/2 tsp lemon zest (optional)
Salt and pepper to taste

INSTRUCTIONS

1. Lay the smoked salmon slices flat on a clean surface.
2. Mix the cream cheese with garlic powder, lemon zest (if using), salt (just a pinch), and pepper.
3. Spread cream cheese mixture (a thin layer) onto each slice of smoked salmon.
4. Roll up the salmon slices tightly to form logs.
5. Slice each roll into bite-sized pieces and serve immediately.

Note: *For a strict carnivore version, omit any garnishes shown in the images.*

NUTRITION

CALORIES: 200, PROTEIN: 18G, CARBOHYDRATES: 1G, FAT: 15G,

GRILLED SHRIMP SKEWERS WITH GARLIC BUTTER

These Grilled Shrimp Skewers with Garlic Butter are a quick and flavorful snack or appetizer. The garlic butter enhances the shrimp's natural sweetness, making this dish a favorite.

PREP TIME: 10 MINS

COOK TIME: 5 MINS

SERVING 2

INGREDIENTS

1/2 lb shrimp, peeled and deveined
2 tbsp butter, melted
1 tsp garlic powder
1/2 tsp smoked paprika
Salt and pepper to taste

INSTRUCTIONS

1. Preheat the grill to medium-high heat.
2. Thread the shrimp and brush them with melted butter. Sprinkle with garlic powder, smoked paprika, salt, and pepper.
3. Grill the skewers for 2–3 minutes on one side until the shrimp are pink and opaque.
4. Drizzle with any leftover melted butter before serving.

Note: For a strict carnivore version, omit any garnishes shown in the images.

NUTRITION

CALORIES: 220, PROTEIN: 25G, CARBOHYDRATES: 0G, FAT: 12G,

CARNIVORE-STYLE DEVILED EGGS

These Carnivore-Style Deviled Eggs are a rich and creamy snack, perfect for any time of the day. Made with just a few ingredients, they're simple yet delicious.

PREP TIME: 10 MINS

COOK TIME: 10 MINS

SERVING 2

INGREDIENTS

4 large eggs
2 tbsp mayonnaise (or mashed egg yolks mixed with butter)
1/2 tsp garlic powder
1/4 tsp smoked paprika
Salt and pepper to taste

Note: *For a strict carnivore version, omit any garnishes shown in the images.*

INSTRUCTIONS

1. Boil the eggs for 8–10 minutes, then transfer to an ice bath. Peel and cut them in lengthwise.
2. Scoop out the yellow part and place them in a bowl. Mash with mayonnaise or butter, garlic powder, smoked paprika, salt, and pepper.
3. Spoon or pipe the yellow egg part mixture back into the egg whites. Spread an additional sprinkle of smoked paprika and serve.

NUTRITION

CALORIES: 180, PROTEIN: 12G, CARBOHYDRATES: 0G, FAT: 15G,

PAN-FRIED SAUSAGE BITES

These Pan-Fried Sausage Bites are a quick and savory snack, perfect for the carnivore diet. The crispy edges and juicy interior make them irresistible.

PREP TIME: 5 MINS

COOK TIME: 10 MINS

SERVING 2

INGREDIENTS

2 sausages (uncooked, your choice)
2 tbsp beef fat (tallow)
1/2 tsp garlic powder
1/4 tsp smoked paprika
Salt and pepper to taste

INSTRUCTIONS

1. Slice the sausages into bite-sized pieces. Heat the beef fat in a skillet.
2. Add sausage bites and sprinkle with garlic powder, smoked paprika, salt, and crushed pepper.
3. Cook for 8–10 minutes, keep stirring occasionally, until the sausage bites are browned and crispy.
4. Serve immediately, optionally drizzled with any leftover fat from the skillet.

Note: *For a strict carnivore version, omit any garnishes shown in the images.*

NUTRITION

CALORIES: 300, PROTEIN: 20G, CARBOHYDRATES: 0G, FAT: 25G,

PORK BELLY CRISPS WITH BEEF FAT GLAZE

Crispy and flavorful, these Pork Belly Crisps with Beef Fat Glaze are a decadent snack. The rich beef fat glaze enhances the crunchy pork belly for a truly indulgent treat.

PREP TIME: 10 MINS

COOK TIME: 15 MINS

SERVING 2

INGREDIENTS

1/2 lb pork belly, thinly sliced
2 tbsp beef fat (tallow)
1/2 tsp garlic powder
1/4 tsp smoked paprika
Salt and pepper to taste

INSTRUCTIONS

1. Preheat a skillet over moderate flame and add one tbsp beef fat.
2. Cook the pork belly slices in batches, 3–4 minutes on one side, until golden brown and crispy. Remove and set aside.
3. Use the same skillet and add leftover beef fat, garlic powder, smoked paprika, salt, and pepper. Stir for 1–2 minutes to create a glaze.
4. Drizzle the beef fat glaze over the pork belly crisps before serving.
5. Serve warm as a crunchy snack or appetizer.

Note: *For a strict carnivore version, omit any garnishes shown in the images.*

NUTRITION

CALORIES: 400, PROTEIN: 15G, CARBOHYDRATES: 0G, FAT: 35G,

SOUPS & BROTHS

BEEF BONE BROTH SOUP

Rich and nourishing, Beef Bone Broth Soup is a cornerstone of the carnivore diet. This warm, flavorful soup is packed with nutrients and perfect for a hearty start to any meal.

PREP TIME: 10 MINS

COOK TIME: 8-12 HOURS

SERVING 4

INGREDIENTS

2 lbs beef bones (marrow or knuckle bones)
3 quarts water
1 tbsp apple cider vinegar (optional)
1 tsp garlic powder
Salt and pepper to taste

Note: *For a strict carnivore version, omit any garnishes shown in the images.*

INSTRUCTIONS

1. Place the beef bones in a stockpot. Cover them with water. Add apple cider vinegar (optional) to help extract nutrients from the bones.
2. Get it to a boil, then decrease the stove heat to simmer. Skim off any foam that rise to the surface.
3. Add garlic powder, salt, and crushed pepper. Cover and simmer for 8–12 hours, checking occasionally to ensure the water level stays above the bones.
4. Strain the broth to discard the solids. Serve hot or store for later use in the fridge.

NUTRITION

CALORIES: 80, PROTEIN: 8G, CARBOHYDRATES: 0G, FAT: 4G,

CREAMY CHICKEN AND EGG DROP SOUP

This Creamy Chicken and Egg Drop Soup is a comforting and protein-rich dish. The delicate egg ribbons and tender chicken make it a satisfying carnivore meal.

PREP TIME: 10 MINS

COOK TIME: 15 MINS

SERVING 4

INGREDIENTS

2 cups shredded cooked chicken
4 cups chicken broth
2 large eggs, beaten
2 tbsp butter
1 tsp garlic powder
Salt and pepper to taste

INSTRUCTIONS

1. Heat the chicken broth in a deep-bottom pot over a moderate flame. Toss in garlic powder, salt, and pepper.
2. Add shredded chicken and cook for 4-5 minutes.
3. Decrease the stove heat to low and slowly drizzle the pulsed eggs into the soup while stirring gently to create ribbons.
4. Toss in the butter until melted and incorporated. Serve hot, optionally garnished with additional melted butter.

Note: *For a strict carnivore version, omit any garnishes shown in the images.*

NUTRITION

CALORIES: 200, PROTEIN: 18G, CARBOHYDRATES: 0G, FAT: 12G,

LAMB SHANK AND BONE MARROW STEW

This Lamb Shank and Bone Marrow Stew is a rich and flavorful dish. The combination of tender lamb and nutrient-dense bone marrow creates a luxurious, carnivore-friendly soup.

PREP TIME: 15 MINS

COOK TIME: 2 HOURS

SERVING 4

INGREDIENTS

2 lamb shanks
2 cups bone marrow (from beef or lamb bones)
4 cups bone broth
2 tbsp butter
1 tsp garlic powder
Salt and pepper to taste

Note: For a strict carnivore version, omit any garnishes shown in the images.

INSTRUCTIONS

1. Heat two tbsp butter in a deep-bottom pot over a moderate flame. Brown the lamb shanks sides, then remove and set aside.
2. Add bone broth to the pot, scraping up any browned bits. Toss in garlic powder, salt, and pepper.
3. Return the lamb shanks and add bone marrow. Get it to a boil, then reduce to a simmer.
4. Cover and cook for 120 minutes until the lamb is tender and the marrow is fully rendered into the broth.
5. Serve hot, with the marrow and broth poured over the lamb shanks.

NUTRITION

CALORIES: 400, PROTEIN: 25G, CARBOHYDRATES: 0G, FAT: 35G,

SHRIMP AND CRAB BISQUE (DAIRY OPTIONAL)

Rich and luxurious, Shrimp and Crab Bisque is a seafood lover's dream. This creamy, savory soup is packed with flavor and can be customized with or without dairy.

PREP TIME: 10 MINS

COOK TIME: 20 MINS

SERVING 4

INGREDIENTS

1/2 lb shrimp, peeled and deveined
1/2 lb crab meat
4 cups seafood broth
2 tbsp butter
1/2 cup heavy cream (optional)
Salt and pepper to taste

INSTRUCTIONS

1. Heat two tbsp butter in a deep-bottom pot over moderate flame. Add shrimp and cook for 2–3 minutes. Remove and set aside.
2. Add seafood broth to the pot and bring to a simmer. Toss in salt and pepper.
3. Blend half of the shrimp and crab meat into the broth for a creamier texture, then return to the pot.
4. Toss in the heavy cream (if using) and simmer for 5 minutes.
5. Serve hot, garnished with the leftover shrimp and crab meat.

Note: *For a strict carnivore version, omit any garnishes shown in the images.*

NUTRITION

CALORIES: 280, PROTEIN: 25G, CARBOHYDRATES: 0G, FAT: 20G,

SPICED DUCK BROTH WITH EGG YOLK SWIRLS

Warm and flavorful, Spiced Duck Broth with Egg Yolk Swirls is a unique carnivore soup. The richness of duck broth combined with the creamy egg yolks makes this a decadent and nourishing option.

PREP TIME: 10 MINS

COOK TIME: 20 MINS

SERVING 4

INGREDIENTS

4 cups duck broth
4 egg yolks
1 tsp garlic powder
1/2 tsp smoked paprika
Salt and pepper to taste

Note: *For a strict carnivore version, omit any garnishes shown in the images.*

INSTRUCTIONS

1. Heat the duck broth in a deep-bottom pot over a moderate flame. Toss in garlic powder, smoked paprika, salt, and pepper.
2. Bring the broth to a gentle simmer.
3. In a small, deep-bottom bowl, whisk the egg yolks until smooth. Slowly drizzle the yolks into the simmering broth, stirring gently to create swirls.
4. Simmer for more 2–3 minutes to set the egg yolks slightly.
5. Serve hot, optionally garnished with a sprinkle of smoked paprika.

NUTRITION

CALORIES: 180, PROTEIN: 10G, CARBOHYDRATES: 0G, FAT: 15G,

SLOW-COOKED OXTAIL SOUP

Deeply flavorful and nutrient-dense, Slow-Cooked Oxtail Soup is a comforting dish that highlights tender, slow-cooked meat and a rich broth. Perfect for a hearty carnivore meal.

PREP TIME: 15 MINS

COOK TIME: 6-8 HOURS

SERVING 4

INGREDIENTS

2 lbs oxtail
4 cups beef broth
2 tbsp butter
1 tsp garlic powder
Salt and pepper to taste

INSTRUCTIONS

1. Heat one tbsp butter in a skillet over moderate flame. Sear the oxtail pieces on all sides, then transfer them to a slow cooker.
2. Add beef broth, garlic powder, salt, and pepper to the slow cooker. Stir to combine.
3. Cover and cook on low for 6–8 hours until the oxtail is tender and the meat falls off the bone.
4. Skim off any excess fat and toss in the leftover butter before serving.
5. Ladle into bowls and serve hot.

Note: *For a strict carnivore version, omit any garnishes shown in the images.*

NUTRITION

CALORIES: 450, PROTEIN: 30G, CARBOHYDRATES: 0G, FAT: 35G,

CREAMY SALMON CHOWDER

Rich and creamy, this Salmon Chowder is a comforting soup packed with the delicate flavors of fresh salmon. Customize with or without dairy to suit your preferences.

PREP TIME: 10 MINS

COOK TIME: 20 MINS

SERVING 4

INGREDIENTS

1 lb salmon fillet, cubed
4 cups fish broth
2 tbsp butter
1/2 cup heavy cream (optional)
Salt and pepper to taste

INSTRUCTIONS

1. Heat one tbsp butter in a deep-bottom pot over moderate flame. Add cubed salmon and sear for 2–3 minutes, then remove and set aside.
2. Add fish broth to the pot and bring to a simmer. Toss in salt and pepper.
3. Return the salmon to the pot and cook for 5 minutes. Toss in heavy cream and leftover butter.
4. Simmer for more 2–3 minutes to allow flavors to meld.
5. Serve hot, optionally garnished with an extra drizzle of melted butter.

Note: *For a strict carnivore version, omit any garnishes shown in the images.*

NUTRITION

CALORIES: 320, PROTEIN: 30G, CARBOHYDRATES: 0G, FAT: 20G,

ROASTED BONE MARROW AND GARLIC SOUP

Roasted Bone Marrow and Garlic Soup is a deeply savory and luxurious dish. The roasted garlic and marrow create a rich and satisfying broth, perfect for a carnivore feast.

PREP TIME: 15 MINS

COOK TIME: 1 HOUR

SERVING 4

INGREDIENTS

1 lb beef marrow bones
4 cups beef broth
2 cloves garlic, roasted
2 tbsp butter
Salt and pepper to taste

INSTRUCTIONS

1. Preheat oven to 400°F (200°C). Place the marrow bones and garlic cloves on the parchment paper-arranged baking sheet. Roast for 30 minutes until the marrow is soft and bubbling.
2. Scoop the marrow out of the bones and mash the roasted garlic into a paste.
3. In a deep-bottom pot, melt the butter over a moderate flame. Add garlic paste and marrow, stirring to combine.
4. Ladle in the beef broth and bring to a simmer. Powder it with salt and crushed pepper.
5. Simmer for 15 minutes, then serve hot.

Note: *For a strict carnivore version, omit any garnishes shown in the images.*

NUTRITION

CALORIES: 300, PROTEIN: 15G, CARBOHYDRATES: 0G, FAT: 25G,

PORK BELLY SOUP WITH CRISPY FAT TOPPING

This Pork Belly Soup with Crispy Fat Topping combines tender pork belly in a rich broth with crispy fat pieces for added texture and flavor. A perfect carnivore comfort food.

PREP TIME: 15 MINS

COOK TIME: 1 HOUR

SERVING 4

INGREDIENTS

1 lb pork belly, cubed
4 cups bone broth
2 tbsp beef fat (tallow)
1/2 tsp garlic powder
Salt and pepper to taste

INSTRUCTIONS

1. Heat one tbsp beef fat in a skillet over moderate flame. Sear the pork belly cubes until golden brown. Remove and set aside.
2. In a deep-bottom pot, add bone broth, garlic powder, salt, and pepper. Bring to a simmer.
3. Add seared pork belly to the broth and simmer for 45 minutes until tender.
4. Heat the leftover beef fat in a skillet and crisp up a few pieces of pork belly fat.
5. Serve the soup hot, garnished with the crispy fat topping.

Note: *For a strict carnivore version, omit any garnishes shown in the images.*

NUTRITION

CALORIES: 400, PROTEIN: 20G, CARBOHYDRATES: 0G, FAT: 35G,

LOBSTER BISQUE WITH CREAMY BUTTER BASE

This luxurious Lobster Bisque with Creamy Butter Base is a rich and indulgent soup. The tender lobster and buttery base create a perfect balance of flavor and texture.

PREP TIME: 15 MINS

COOK TIME: 25 MINS

SERVING 4

INGREDIENTS

1 lb lobster meat, chopped
4 cups seafood broth
4 tbsp butter
1/2 cup heavy cream (optional)
Salt and pepper to taste

INSTRUCTIONS

1. Heat 2 tbsp butter in a deep-bottom pot over moderate flame. Add lobster meat and cook for 2–3 minutes, then remove and set aside.
2. Add seafood broth to the pot and bring to a simmer. Powder it with salt and crushed pepper.
3. Blend half of the lobster meat with a small amount of broth for a creamy texture, then return to the pot.
4. Toss in the heavy cream (if using) and the leftover butter. Simmer for 5 minutes.
5. Serve hot, garnished with the reserved lobster meat.

Note: *For a strict carnivore version, omit any garnishes shown in the images.*

NUTRITION

CALORIES: 350, PROTEIN: 30G, CARBOHYDRATES: 0G, FAT: 25G,

APPETIZERS & STARTERS

SEARED SCALLOPS IN GARLIC BUTTER

Delicate and flavorful, Seared Scallops in Garlic Butter make for a perfect carnivore appetizer. The golden crust paired with rich garlic butter elevates this dish to a fine dining experience.

PREP TIME: 5 MINS

COOK TIME: 5 MINS

SERVING 2

INGREDIENTS

8 large scallops
2 tbsp butter
1 clove garlic, mashed
1/2 tsp smoked paprika
Salt and pepper to taste

INSTRUCTIONS

1. Pat the scallops dry and massage with salt, pepper, and smoked paprika.
2. Heat two tbsp butter in a skillet over moderate flame. Add mashed garlic and sauté for 30 seconds until fragrant.
3. Place the scallops in the skillet and sear for 2 minutes on one side without moving them.
4. Flip the scallops and cook for more 1–2 minutes until golden brown and opaque.
5. Remove from heat and drizzle with the garlic butter from the skillet. Serve immediately.

Note: *For a strict carnivore version, omit any garnishes shown in the images.*

NUTRITION

CALORIES: 220, PROTEIN: 25G, CARBOHYDRATES: 0G, FAT: 12G,

CARNIVORE MEATBALLS

These Carnivore Meatballs are juicy, high-fat, and packed with rich flavor. Made with minimal ingredients, they're the perfect meaty appetizer or snack!

PREP TIME: 10 MINS

COOK TIME: 10 MINS

SERVING 4

INGREDIENTS

1 lb ground beef
1 large egg
2 tbsp beef tallow
1 tsp sea salt
1/2 tsp black pepper

INSTRUCTIONS

1. In a bowl, mix ground beef, egg, salt, and pepper until well combined.
2. Shape the mixture into small meatballs (about 1-inch in diameter).
3. Heat beef tallow in a skillet over medium heat.
4. Add meatballs and cook for 3-4 minutes per side until browned and cooked through.
5. Remove from heat and let rest for 2 minutes before serving.

Note: *For a strict carnivore version, omit any garnishes shown in the images.*

NUTRITION

CALORIES: 380, PROTEIN: 28G, CARBOHYDRATES: 0G, FAT: 30G,

BUTTER-FRIED CHICKEN LIVERS

Rich in flavor and nutrients, these Butter-Fried Chicken Livers are crispy on the outside and tender inside, making them the perfect carnivore-friendly starter.

PREP TIME: 10 MINS

COOK TIME: 10 MINS

SERVING 4

INGREDIENTS

8 oz chicken livers
3 tbsp butter
1 tsp sea salt
1/2 tsp black pepper

INSTRUCTIONS

1. Heat butter in a skillet over medium-high heat until melted.
2. Add chicken livers and season with salt and pepper.
3. Sear for 2-3 minutes per side until golden brown and crispy.
4. Reduce heat and cook for another 3-4 minutes until fully cooked but still tender inside.
5. Remove from heat and serve warm.

Note: *For a strict carnivore version, omit any garnishes shown in the images.*

NUTRITION

CALORIES: 320, PROTEIN: 28G, CARBOHYDRATES: 0G, FAT: 22G,

SMOKED SALMON BITES WITH CREAM CHEESE

These Smoked Salmon Bites with Cream Cheese are a delightful and elegant carnivore-friendly appetizer. The creamy cheese complements the smoky salmon perfectly.

PREP TIME: 10 MINS

COOK TIME: 00 MINS

SERVING 2

INGREDIENTS

4 oz smoked salmon
2 oz cream cheese, softened
1/2 tsp lemon zest (optional)
Salt and pepper to taste

INSTRUCTIONS

1. Cut the smoked salmon into bite-sized pieces.
2. Mix the cream cheese with lemon zest, salt, and pepper until smooth.
3. Spread cream cheese (a small amount) onto each piece of smoked salmon.
4. Roll up the salmon or fold it into small bundles.
5. Arrange on a plate and serve chilled.

Note: *For a strict carnivore version, omit any garnishes shown in the images.*

NUTRITION
CALORIES: 200, PROTEIN: 18G, CARBOHYDRATES: 1G, FAT: 15G,

CRISPY CHICKEN WINGS WITH BUTTER DIP

Crispy Chicken Wings with Butter Dip are a crowd-pleasing appetizer. The golden, crispy wings paired with a rich, buttery dip make for a flavorful and satisfying treat.

PREP TIME: 5 MINS

COOK TIME: 40 MINS

SERVING 4

INGREDIENTS

2 lbs chicken wings
2 tbsp butter
1/2 tsp garlic powder
Salt and pepper to taste

INSTRUCTIONS

1. Preheat oven to 400°F (200°C). Arrange the baking sheet with parchment paper.
2. Pat the chicken wings dry and season with garlic powder, salt, and pepper. Arrange on the parchment paper-arranged baking sheet in one layer (don't overlap).
3. Bake for 35–40 minutes, flip after halftime has passed, until golden and crispy.
4. In a small saucepan, melt the butter and season with salt (just a pinch).
5. Serve the crispy wings hot with the butter dip on the side.

Note: *For a strict carnivore version, omit any garnishes shown in the images.*

NUTRITION

CALORIES: 350, PROTEIN: 30G, CARBOHYDRATES: 0G, FAT: 25G,

GRILLED SHRIMP SKEWERS IN HERB BUTTER

Juicy and tender, these Grilled Shrimp Skewers in Herb Butter are a quick and flavorful appetizer. The herb butter enhances the natural sweetness of the shrimp for a delicious bite.

PREP TIME: 10 MINS

COOK TIME: 5 MINS

SERVING 2

INGREDIENTS

1/2 lb shrimp, peeled and deveined

2 tbsp butter, melted

1 tsp fresh parsley, chopped (optional)

1/2 tsp garlic powder

Salt and pepper to taste

Note: *For a strict carnivore version, omit any garnishes shown in the images.*

INSTRUCTIONS

1. Preheat grill to medium-high heat.
2. Thread the shrimp and brush with melted butter. Sprinkle with garlic powder, salt, and pepper.
3. Grill the skewers for 2–3 minutes on one side until the shrimp are pink and opaque.
4. Remove from the grill and drizzle with any leftover melted butter. Spread parsley if desired.
5. Serve hot as a flavorful appetizer.

NUTRITION

CALORIES: 220, PROTEIN: 25G, CARBOHYDRATES: 0G, FAT: 12G,

BACON-WRAPPED CHEESE BITES (OPTIONAL DAIRY)

These Bacon-Wrapped Cheese Bites are a rich and indulgent snack. The crispy bacon perfectly complements the gooey, melted cheese, making them irresistible for carnivore eaters.

PREP TIME: 10 MINS

COOK TIME: 10 MINS

SERVING 2

INGREDIENTS

4 oz cheese, cut into cubes (optional)
8 slices of bacon
1/2 tsp smoked paprika
Salt and pepper to taste

Note: *For a strict carnivore version, omit any garnishes shown in the images.*

INSTRUCTIONS

1. Preheat oven to 400°F (200°C). Arrange the baking sheet with parchment paper.
2. Wrap each cheese cube with a slice of bacon, securing it with a toothstick if necessary.
3. Place the bacon-wrapped bites on the parchment paper-arranged baking sheet and sprinkle with smoked paprika.
4. Bake for 7-10 minutes until the bacon is crispy.
5. Let cool slightly before serving to prevent the cheese from spilling out.

NUTRITION

CALORIES: 300, PROTEIN: 20G, CARBOHYDRATES: 0G, FAT: 25G,

FRIED PORK BELLY CUBES WITH GARLIC BUTTER

Crispy on the outside and tender on the inside, these Fried Pork Belly Cubes with Garlic Butter are a savory and satisfying appetizer. The garlic butter adds a rich and flavorful finish.

PREP TIME: 10 MINS

COOK TIME: 15 MINS

SERVING 2

INGREDIENTS

1/2 lb pork belly, cubed
2 tbsp butter
1/2 tsp garlic powder
Salt and pepper to taste

INSTRUCTIONS

1. Heat a skillet over moderate flame and add pork belly cubes. Cook for 8–10 minutes, stirring occasionally, until crispy and golden brown.
2. Remove the pork belly cubes and set aside.
3. Use the same skillet, melt the butter, and toss in garlic powder, salt, and pepper.
4. Return the pork belly cubes and toss well to coat them in the garlic butter.
5. Serve hot as a crunchy and flavorful appetizer.

Note: *For a strict carnivore version, omit any garnishes shown in the images.*

NUTRITION

CALORIES: 400, PROTEIN: 15G, CARBOHYDRATES: 0G, FAT: 35G,

GRILLED LAMB CHOPS WITH MINT BUTTER

These Grilled Lamb Chops with Mint Butter are a sophisticated appetizer bursting with flavor. The mint butter enhances the rich, tender lamb for a memorable dish.

PREP TIME: 10 MINS

COOK TIME: 10 MINS

SERVING 2

INGREDIENTS

4 lamb chops
2 tbsp butter, softened
1 tsp fresh mint, chopped (optional)
1/2 tsp garlic powder
Salt and pepper to taste

Note: *For a strict carnivore version, omit any garnishes shown in the images.*

INSTRUCTIONS

1. Preheat grill to medium-high heat. Massage the lamb chops with garlic powder, salt, and pepper.
2. Grill the chops for 4–5 minutes on one side until they reach your desired level of doneness.
3. In a small, deep-bottom bowl, mix the softened butter with chopped mint.
4. Spread the mint butter over the lamb chops as they rest for 5 minutes.
5. Serve hot, garnished with additional mint if desired.

NUTRITION

CALORIES: 350, PROTEIN: 25G, CARBOHYDRATES: 0G, FAT: 28G,

CRISPY DUCK BREAST BITES WITH SAVORY GLAZE

Crispy Duck Breast Bites with Savory Glaze are a flavorful and elegant appetizer. The crispy skin and rich glaze make this dish a standout for any occasion.

PREP TIME: 10 MINS

COOK TIME: 15 MINS

SERVING 2

INGREDIENTS

1 duck breast, diced
2 tbsp butter
1/2 cup bone broth
1/2 tsp garlic powder
Salt and pepper to taste

INSTRUCTIONS

1. Heat a skillet over moderate flame. Place the diced duck breast skin-side down in the skillet and cook for 4–5 minutes until the skin is crispy. Flip and cook for more 2–3 minutes.
2. Remove the duck breast bites and set aside.
3. Use the same skillet and add butter and bone broth. Toss in garlic powder, salt, and pepper. Simmer for 3–4 minutes to decrease the sauce slightly.
4. Return the duck bites to the skillet and toss to coat them in the glaze.
5. Serve hot, drizzled with any leftover sauce.

Note: *For a strict carnivore version, omit any garnishes shown in the images.*

NUTRITION
CALORIES: 350, PROTEIN: 25G, CARBOHYDRATES: 0G, FAT: 28G,

SIDE DISHES

BACON-WRAPPED SAUSAGE BITES

These Bacon-Wrapped Sausage Bites are crispy, juicy, and packed with flavor. The perfect high-fat, protein-rich carnivore side dish or snack, these bite-sized treats are simple to make and absolutely delicious!

PREP TIME: 10 MINS

COOK TIME: 20 MINS

SERVING 2

INGREDIENTS

8 small sausage links (or cut large sausages into bite-sized pieces)
8 slices bacon
1 tsp sea salt
1/2 tsp black pepper

INSTRUCTIONS

1. Preheat oven to 400°F (200°C).
2. Wrap each sausage link tightly with a slice of bacon.
3. Place wrapped sausages on a baking sheet, seam side down.
4. Bake for 18-20 minutes, flipping halfway, until bacon is crispy.
5. Remove from oven, let cool for a minute, and serve warm.

Note: *For a strict carnivore version, omit any garnishes shown in the images.*

NUTRITION

CALORIES: 420, PROTEIN: 32G, CARBOHYDRATES: 0G, FAT: 35G,

BUTTER-ROASTED CHICKEN THIGHS

Juicy and flavorful, Butter-Roasted Chicken Thighs are a versatile side dish that pairs well with any carnivore meal. The butter enhances the natural flavors of the chicken.

PREP TIME: 10 MINS

COOK TIME: 30 MINS

SERVING 2

INGREDIENTS

4 chicken thighs (bone-in, skin-on)
3 tbsp butter
1 tsp garlic powder
Salt and pepper to taste

INSTRUCTIONS

1. Preheat oven to 400°F (200°C).
2. Pat the chicken thighs dry and powder it with garlic powder, salt, and pepper.
3. Melt the butter over moderate flame. Place the thighs skin-side down and sear for 3–4 minutes until golden brown.
4. Flip the thighs and transfer the skillet to the oven. Roast for 25–30 minutes until the food thermometer shows internal temperature readings of 165°F.
5. Serve hot, drizzled with the buttery pan drippings.

Note: *For a strict carnivore version, omit any garnishes shown in the images.*

NUTRITION

CALORIES: 350, PROTEIN: 25G, CARBOHYDRATES: 0G, FAT: 28G,

GRILLED CHICKEN TENDERS

These Grilled Chicken Tenders are juicy, flavorful, and seared to perfection. With a simple seasoning of salt and pepper, they let the natural richness of the chicken shine. Perfect as a side dish or a protein-packed snack!

PREP TIME: 10 MINS

COOK TIME: 10 MINS

SERVING 4

INGREDIENTS

1 lb chicken tenders
2 tbsp beef tallow (or butter)
1 tsp sea salt
1/2 tsp black pepper

INSTRUCTIONS

1. Preheat a grill or grill pan to medium-high heat.
2. Brush chicken tenders with melted beef tallow and season with salt and pepper.
3. Grill for 4-5 minutes per side until golden brown and cooked through.
4. Remove from heat and let rest for 2 minutes before serving.

Note: *For a strict carnivore version, omit any garnishes shown in the images.*

NUTRITION

CALORIES: 250, PROTEIN: 35G, CARBOHYDRATES: 0G, FAT: 22G,

PORK BELLY STRIPS WITH HERB BUTTER GLAZE

Pork Belly Strips with Herb Butter Glaze are crispy and flavorful, making them a perfect carnivore side dish. The herb butter adds a rich and aromatic finish.

PREP TIME: 10 MINS

COOK TIME: 15 MINS

SERVING 2

INGREDIENTS

1/2 lb pork belly, sliced
2 tbsp butter
1 tsp fresh rosemary or thyme, chopped (optional)
1/2 tsp garlic powder
Salt and pepper to taste

INSTRUCTIONS

1. Heat a skillet over moderate flame. Add pork belly strips and cook for 6–8 minutes on one side until crispy. Remove and set aside.
2. Use the same skillet, melt the butter, and toss in the chopped herbs, garlic powder, salt, and pepper.
3. Return the pork belly strips to the skillet and toss to coat them in the herb butter glaze.
4. Serve hot, spread additional herbs on top if desired.

Note: *For a strict carnivore version, omit any garnishes shown in the images.*

NUTRITION

CALORIES: 400, PROTEIN: 15G, CARBOHYDRATES: 0G, FAT: 35G,

BEEF STEAK BITES

These Beef Steak Bites are seared in beef tallow for a crispy crust and juicy center. Packed with rich flavor, they're a perfect high-protein, high-fat side dish or snack!

PREP TIME: 10 MINS

COOK TIME: 20 MINS

SERVING 4

INGREDIENTS

1 lb ribeye or sirloin steak, cut into bite-sized cubes
2 tbsp beef tallow
1 tsp sea salt
1/2 tsp black pepper

INSTRUCTIONS

1. Heat beef tallow in a skillet over high heat.
2. Season steak bites with salt and pepper.
3. Add steak bites to the skillet and sear for 2-3 minutes per side until golden brown.
4. Remove from heat and let rest for 2 minutes before serving.

Note: *For a strict carnivore version, omit any garnishes shown in the images.*

NUTRITION

CALORIES: 380, PROTEIN: 40G, CARBOHYDRATES: 1G, FAT: 25G,

PAN-SEARED LAMB CHOPS WITH GARLIC BUTTER

Tender and flavorful, these Pan-Seared Lamb Chops with Garlic Butter are a quick and elegant carnivore-friendly side dish. The rich garlic butter enhances the natural juiciness of the lamb.

PREP TIME: 10 MINS

COOK TIME: 10 MINS

SERVING 2

INGREDIENTS

- 4 lamb chops
- 2 tbsp butter
- 1/2 tsp garlic powder
- Salt and pepper to taste

INSTRUCTIONS

1. Massage the lamb chops with garlic powder, salt, and pepper.
2. Heat a skillet over moderate flame and add one tbsp butter.
3. Place the chops to sear in a skillet for 3–4 minutes on one side.
4. Remove the lamb chops and let rest for 5 minutes.
5. Melt the leftover butter in the skillet, toss in the browned bits, and drizzle over the lamb chops before serving.

Note: *For a strict carnivore version, omit any garnishes shown in the images.*

NUTRITION

CALORIES: 350, PROTEIN: 25G, CARBOHYDRATES: 0G, FAT: 28G,

GRILLED SALMON WITH BONE BROTH REDUCTION

Grilled Salmon with Bone Broth Reduction is a light yet rich side dish. The bone broth reduction enhances the salmon's natural flavor, creating a perfectly balanced dish.

PREP TIME: 5 MINS

COOK TIME: 15 MINS

SERVING 2

INGREDIENTS

2 salmon fillets (6 oz each)
1 cup bone broth
2 tbsp butter
Salt and pepper to taste

INSTRUCTIONS

1. Preheat the grill to medium-high heat. Massage the salmon fillets with salt and pepper.
2. Grill the fish fillet skin-side down for 6–8 minutes, then flip and grill for more 2–3 minutes until cooked through.
3. In a small saucepan, simmer the bone broth over moderate flame until reduced by half. Toss in the butter to create a smooth sauce.
4. Serve the grilled salmon with the bone broth reduction drizzled over the top.

Note: *For a strict carnivore version, omit any garnishes shown in the images.*

NUTRITION

CALORIES: 300, PROTEIN: 30G, CARBOHYDRATES: 0G, FAT: 20G,

SCRAMBLED EGG AND PORK BELLY MIX

Scrambled Egg and Pork Belly Mix is a hearty and flavorful side dish that combines crispy pork belly with creamy scrambled eggs for a delicious carnivore option.

PREP TIME: 5 MINS

COOK TIME: 10 MINS

SERVING 2

INGREDIENTS

4 large eggs
1/2 lb pork belly, cubed
2 tbsp butter
Salt and pepper to taste

INSTRUCTIONS

1. Heat a skillet over moderate flame and add pork belly cubes. Cook for 6–8 minutes until crispy, then remove and set aside.
2. Use the same skillet and melt the butter over low heat.
3. Beat the eggs in a bowl and ladle into the skillet. Stir gently to create soft curds.
4. Add crispy pork belly back to the skillet and fold into the scrambled eggs.
5. Serve hot as a rich and satisfying side dish.

Note: *For a strict carnivore version, omit any garnishes shown in the images.*

NUTRITION
CALORIES: 400, PROTEIN: 25G, CARBOHYDRATES: 0G, FAT: 35G,

BUTTER-BASTED SCALLOPS AS A SIDE DISH

These Butter-Basted Scallops are a simple yet luxurious, carnivore-friendly side dish. The rich, buttery flavor complements the delicate texture of the scallops.

PREP TIME: 5 MINS

COOK TIME: 5 MINS

SERVING 2

INGREDIENTS

8 large scallops
2 tbsp butter
1/2 tsp garlic powder
Salt and pepper to taste

INSTRUCTIONS

1. Pat the scallops dry and season with garlic powder, salt, and pepper.
2. Heat two tbsp butter in a skillet over moderate flame until foamy.
3. Add scallops and cook for 2 minutes on one side.
4. Flip the scallops and spoon the melted butter over them for more 1–2 minutes until golden and opaque.
5. Serve hot, drizzled with the leftover butter.

Note: *For a strict carnivore version, omit any garnishes shown in the images.*

NUTRITION
CALORIES: 220, PROTEIN: 25G, CARBOHYDRATES: 0G, FAT: 12G,

CRISPY CHICKEN FAT BITES

These Crispy Chicken Fat Bites are packed with flavor, providing a crunchy, high-fat snack or side dish that's perfect for the carnivore diet. Fried in beef tallow, they deliver deep richness and a satisfying bite.

PREP TIME: 5 MINS

COOK TIME: 15 MINS

SERVING 4

INGREDIENTS

12 oz chicken fat (skin or trimmings, cut into small pieces)
2 tbsp beef tallow
1 tsp sea salt
1/2 tsp black pepper

INSTRUCTIONS

1. Heat beef tallow in a skillet over medium heat.
2. Add chicken fat pieces and cook, stirring occasionally, for 8-10 minutes until they start crisping up.
3. Increase heat to medium-high and fry for another 3-5 minutes until golden brown and crunchy.
4. Remove from heat, drain on a paper towel, and season with salt and pepper.
5. Serve warm as a snack or side dish.

Note: *For a strict carnivore version, omit any garnishes shown in the images.*

NUTRITION

CALORIES: 420, PROTEIN: 5G, CARBOHYDRATES: 0G, FAT: 45G,

DESSERTS

EGG CUSTARD WITH HEAVY CREAM

Smooth and rich, Egg Custard with Heavy Cream is a classic carnivore-friendly dessert. This creamy treat is simple to prepare and perfectly indulgent.

PREP TIME: 10 MINS

COOK TIME: 25 MINS

SERVING 4

INGREDIENTS

4 large eggs
1 cup heavy cream
1/2 tsp vanilla extract (optional)
1/2 tsp ground nutmeg (optional)
Salt to taste

Note: *For a strict carnivore version, omit any garnishes shown in the images.*

INSTRUCTIONS

1. Preheat oven to 325°F (160°C). Grab the shallow bowl and toss the eggs, heavy cream, vanilla extract (if using), and salt (just a pinch).
2. Pour the mixture into four small ramekins.
3. Place the ramekins in an oven dish and fill the oven dish with hot water until it stands halfway up the sides of the ramekins.
4. Bake for 25 minutes or until the custard is set but still slightly jiggly in the center.
5. Let cool slightly before serving, optionally sprinkled with ground nutmeg.

NUTRITION
CALORIES: 220, PROTEIN: 6G, CARBOHYDRATES: 1G, FAT: 20G,

WHIPPED CREAM CHEESE MOUSSE

This Whipped Cream Cheese Mousse is a light and creamy dessert that satisfies cravings while staying within the carnivore guidelines. Optional sweeteners can be added for extra flavor.

PREP TIME: 5 MINS

COOK TIME: 00 MINS

SERVING 2

INGREDIENTS

4 oz cream cheese, softened
1/2 cup heavy cream
1/2 tsp vanilla extract (optional)
Sweetener of choice (optional, for non-strict carnivores)
Salt to taste

INSTRUCTIONS

1. Grab the shallow bowl and whip the heavy cream until stiff peaks form.
2. Take the other shallow bowl and beat the cream cheese until smooth and fluffy.
3. Toss whipped cream with the cream cheese mixture until well combined. Add vanilla extract and sweetener (if using).
4. Spoon into serving dishes and chill for 10 minutes before serving.

Note: *For a strict carnivore version, omit any garnishes shown in the images.*

NUTRITION

CALORIES: 300, PROTEIN: 4G, CARBOHYDRATES: 1G, FAT: 30G,

CARNIVORE PANNA COTTA

This Carnivore Panna Cotta is a silky, creamy dessert made with heavy cream and gelatin, delivering a perfect high-fat treat.

PREP TIME: 5 MINS

COOK TIME: 10 MINS

SERVING 4

INGREDIENTS

- 2 cups heavy cream
- 2 tbsp butter
- 1 tbsp gelatin
- 1/2 tsp sea salt

INSTRUCTIONS

1. In a saucepan, heat the heavy cream and butter over low heat until warm.
2. Sprinkle gelatin over the mixture and whisk until fully dissolved.
3. Remove from heat and let cool slightly.
4. Pour into small ramekins or molds and refrigerate for at least 3 hours until set.
5. Serve chilled and enjoy.

Note: *For a strict carnivore version, omit any garnishes shown in the images.*

NUTRITION

CALORIES: 380, PROTEIN: 5G, CARBOHYDRATES: 0G, FAT: 40G,

FROZEN BUTTER BITES WITH VANILLA FLAVORING

Frozen Butter Bites with Vanilla Flavoring are a quick and easy carnivore dessert. These creamy, buttery bites melt in your mouth and make a delightful treat.

PREP TIME: 5 MINS

COOK TIME: 00 MINS

SERVING 4

INGREDIENTS

4 tbsp butter, softened
1 tbsp heavy cream
1/2 tsp vanilla extract
Sweetener of choice (optional)
Salt to taste

INSTRUCTIONS

1. Grab the shallow bowl and whip the butter, heavy cream, vanilla extract, and salt (just a pinch) until light and fluffy. Add sweetener if desired.
2. Spoon the mixture into silicone molds or onto a parchment-lined tray in small dollops.
3. Freeze for 20 minutes until firm.
4. Remove from the molds and serve immediately, or store in the freezer for later.

Note: *For a strict carnivore version, omit any garnishes shown in the images.*

NUTRITION
CALORIES: 100, PROTEIN: 0G, CARBOHYDRATES: 0G, FAT: 11G,

CREAMY EGG PUDDING

Creamy Egg Pudding is a smooth and rich carnivore dessert made with simple ingredients. It is both satisfying and nourishing.

PREP TIME: 10 MINS

COOK TIME: 15 MINS

SERVING 4

INGREDIENTS

4 large eggs
1/2 cup heavy cream (for non-dairy use coconut cream)
1/2 tsp vanilla extract (optional)
Sweetener of choice (optional)
Salt to taste

INSTRUCTIONS

1. Grab the shallow bowl and toss the eggs, heavy cream, vanilla extract, and salt (just a pinch) until smooth.
2. Ladle the mixture into a saucepan and cook over low flame, keep stirring constantly, until thickened, about 10–15 minutes.
3. Remove and ladle into serving dishes. Cool slightly at least 30 minutes.
4. Serve chilled, and enjoy this creamy dessert.

Note: *For a strict carnivore version, omit any garnishes shown in the images.*

NUTRITION

CALORIES: 200, PROTEIN: 6G, CARBOHYDRATES: 1G, FAT: 18G,

KETO CARNIVORE ICE CREAM

Rich and creamy, this Keto Carnivore Ice Cream is made with simple ingredients like eggs and cream. It's a decadent dessert that satisfies cravings while staying carnivore-friendly.

PREP TIME: 10 MINS

COOK TIME: 10 MINS

SERVING 4

INGREDIENTS

4 egg yolks
1 cup heavy cream
1/2 tsp vanilla extract (optional)
Sweetener of choice (optional)
Pinch of salt

Note: *For a strict carnivore version, omit any garnishes shown in the images.*

INSTRUCTIONS

1. In a saucepan, whisk the egg yolks, heavy cream, vanilla extract, and salt (just a pinch). Add sweetener if desired.
2. Cook over low heat, and keep stirring constantly until the mixture gets the thickened slightly and coats the back of a spoon.
3. Remove from heat and let cool completely.
4. Throw the mixture into an ice cream machine and churn as manufacturer's directions. Alternatively, freeze in a shallow dish, stirring every 30 minutes for 2 hours.
5. Serve immediately or store in the freezer.

NUTRITION

CALORIES: 200, PROTEIN: 4G, CARBOHYDRATES: 1G, FAT: 20G,

CREAM CHEESE AND EGG SOUFFLÉ

Light and fluffy, this Cream Cheese and Egg Soufflé is an elegant carnivore dessert. The combination of eggs and cream cheese creates a delicate and airy treat.

PREP TIME: 10 MINS

COOK TIME: 20 MINS

SERVING 4

INGREDIENTS

4 large eggs, separated
4 oz cream cheese, softened
1/2 tsp vanilla extract (optional)
Sweetener of choice (optional)
Pinch of salt

INSTRUCTIONS

1. Preheat oven to 375°F (190°C). Grease four ramekins.
2. Grab the shallow bowl and beat the egg whites with salt (just a pinch) until stiff peaks form.
3. Take the other shallow bowl and mix the egg yolks with cream cheese, vanilla extract, and sweetener (if using) until smooth.
4. Gently fold the egg white and yolk mixture until fully combined.
5. Divide the mixture evenly and bake for 15–20 minutes. Serve immediately.

Note: *For a strict carnivore version, omit any garnishes shown in the images.*

NUTRITION

CALORIES: 180, PROTEIN: 8G, CARBOHYDRATES: 1G, FAT: 16G,

CARNIVORE CHOCOLATE MOUSSE

This Carnivore Chocolate Mousse is a decadent and rich dessert. Made with cocoa powder, it's a perfect treat for those who prefer a dairy-optional and sweetener-free dessert.

PREP TIME: 5 MINS

COOK TIME: 00 MINS

SERVING 4

INGREDIENTS

4 oz cream cheese or coconut cream
1/4 cup heavy cream (optional)
2 tbsp unsweetened cocoa powder
Sweetener of choice (optional)
Pinch of salt

Note: *For a strict carnivore version, omit any garnishes shown in the images.*

INSTRUCTIONS

1. Grab the shallow bowl and beat the cream cheese or coconut cream until smooth and fluffy.
2. Add cocoa powder, heavy cream (if using), and sweetener (if desired). Mix until fully combined and smooth.
3. Ladle the mousse into serving dishes and chill for 10 minutes before serving.
4. Optionally dusting the cocoa powder or a dollop of whipped cream.

NUTRITION
CALORIES: 200, PROTEIN: 4G, CARBOHYDRATES: 2G, FAT: 18G, FIBER: 1G

SALTED CARAMEL EGG CUSTARD

Smooth and indulgent, this Salted Caramel Egg Custard is a creamy carnivore dessert. The salted caramel flavor pairs beautifully with the rich egg custard base.

PREP TIME: 10 MINS

COOK TIME: 25 MINS

SERVING 4

INGREDIENTS

4 large eggs
1 cup heavy cream
1/2 tsp vanilla extract (optional)
Sweetener of choice (optional)
Pinch of sea salt

INSTRUCTIONS

1. Preheat oven to 325°F (160°C). In a deep-bottom bowl, toss the eggs, heavy cream, vanilla extract, and sweetener (if using).
2. Pour the mixture into four ramekins. Sprinkle sea salt (just a pinch) on top of each.
3. Place the ramekins in the oven dish and fill the oven dish with hot water halfway up the sides of the ramekins.
4. Bake for 25 minutes until the custard is set but still slightly jiggly in the center.
5. Cool before serving, optionally garnished with an additional sprinkle of sea salt.

Note: *For a strict carnivore version, omit any garnishes shown in the images.*

NUTRITION

CALORIES: 220, PROTEIN: 6G, CARBOHYDRATES: 1G, FAT: 20G,

SALTED BUTTER FUDGE

This Salted Butter Fudge is rich, creamy, and melts in your mouth. Made with just butter, heavy cream, and a pinch of salt, it's the perfect high-fat carnivore treat!

PREP TIME: 5 MINS

COOK TIME: 10 MINS

SERVING 2

INGREDIENTS

1 cup butter
1/2 cup heavy cream
1/2 tsp sea salt

INSTRUCTIONS

1. In a saucepan over low heat, melt the butter and stir in the heavy cream.
2. Simmer for 5-7 minutes, stirring constantly, until thickened.
3. Pour the mixture into a lined dish and sprinkle with sea salt.
4. Refrigerate for 2 hours until firm.
5. Cut into small squares and enjoy chilled.

Note: *For a strict carnivore version, omit any garnishes shown in the images.*

NUTRITION

CALORIES: 220, PROTEIN: 1G, CARBOHYDRATES: 0G, FAT: 24G,

DRINKS

BONE BROTH LATTE WITH BUTTER

Rich and comforting, this Bone Broth Latte with Butter is prepared entirely from scratch, starting with a homemade bone broth. The creamy butter enhances the natural flavor of the broth for a nourishing and satisfying drink.

PREP TIME: 15 MINS

COOK TIME: 8 HOURS

SERVING: 2

INGREDIENTS

2 lbs beef bones (marrow, knuckle, or joint bones)
8 cups water
1 tbsp apple cider vinegar
2 tbsp butter
1/2 tsp garlic powder (optional)
Pinch of sea salt

INSTRUCTIONS

1. Rinse the beef bones under cold water to remove impurities and place them in a deep-bottom pot or slow cooker.
2. Add 8 cups of water and one tbsp apple cider vinegar, letting the mixture sit for 15–20 minutes to extract nutrients from the bones.
3. Get this mixture to a boil over high heat, then reduce to a low simmer, skimming off any foam or impurities that rise to the surface. Cover and simmer for 8–12 hours, checking occasionally to ensure the bones remain submerged and adding water as needed.
4. Strain the broth through a fine mesh sieve to remove the bones and solids, reserving 2 cups for the latte and storing the rest for later use.
5. Heat 1 cup of the prepared broth in a small saucepan over moderate flame. Add 1 tbsp butter and optional garlic powder, whisking vigorously until the butter melts and the mixture becomes frothy.
6. Pour the prepared broth into a mug, sprinkle with sea salt (just a pinch), and serve hot. Repeat the process with the leftover broth and butter for the second serving.

NUTRITION

CALORIES: 200, PROTEIN: 10G, CARBOHYDRATES: 0G, FAT: 18G,

WHIPPED CREAM COFFEE

Whipped Cream Coffee is a creamy and luxurious drink that's perfect for mornings or a midday pick-me-up. With optional dairy, it's customizable for every carnivore's preferences.

PREP TIME: 5 MINS

COOK TIME: 00 MINS

SERVING 1

INGREDIENTS

1 cup brewed coffee
2 tbsp heavy cream (or coconut cream for non-dairy)
1 tbsp butter
Sweetener of choice (optional)

INSTRUCTIONS

1. Brew a fresh cup coffee.
2. In a small, deep-bottom bowl, whip the heavy cream (or coconut cream) with a whisk until it thickens slightly.
3. Add brewed coffee to a powerful food blender along with the butter and whipped cream.
4. Blend on full power for 30 seconds until the mixture becomes frothy.
5. Ladle into a mug and add sweetener if desired. Serve immediately.
6. Enjoy the rich, creamy flavors of this carnivore-friendly coffee.

NUTRITION

CALORIES: 150, PROTEIN: 1G, CARBOHYDRATES: 0G, FAT: 15G,

SALTED BEEF TEA (WARM BROTH DRINK)

Salted Beef Tea is a warm, savory drink made from beef broth. It's simple, nutrient-packed, and a comforting choice for carnivore enthusiasts.

PREP TIME: 5 MINS

COOK TIME: 5 MINS

SERVING 1

INGREDIENTS

1 cup beef broth
1 tbsp beef fat (tallow)
Pinch of sea salt
1/4 tsp smoked paprika (optional)

INSTRUCTIONS

1. Heat the beef broth over moderate flame until warm.
2. Add beef fat to the broth and whisk until fully melted and incorporated.
3. Powder it with a pinch sea salt and smoked paprika if desired.
4. Ladle the mixture into a mug and stir gently to combine.
5. Serve immediately as a comforting and savory drink.
6. Sip slowly and enjoy the richness of the warm beef tea.

NUTRITION

CALORIES: 100, PROTEIN: 10G, CARBOHYDRATES: 0G, FAT: 8G,

CARNIVORE MILKSHAKE

This Carnivore Milkshake is a rich and creamy drink made with eggs, cream, and butter. Perfect for a high-fat, nutrient-dense treat.

PREP TIME: 5 MINS

COOK TIME: 00 MINS

SERVING 1

INGREDIENTS

2 large eggs
1/2 cup heavy cream
1 tbsp butter, melted
1/2 tsp vanilla extract (optional)
Sweetener of choice (optional)

INSTRUCTIONS

1. Crack the eggs into a powerful food blender and add heavy cream, melted butter, and vanilla extract if desired.
2. Blend on full power until the mixture is smooth and frothy.
3. Add sweetener if desired and blend again briefly.
4. Pour the milkshake into a tall glass.
5. Serve immediately as a creamy, satisfying drink.
6. Enjoy the decadent flavors of this carnivore-friendly milkshake.

NUTRITION

CALORIES: 300, PROTEIN: 8G, CARBOHYDRATES: 1G, FAT: 28G,

CARNIVORE BULLETPROOF COFFEE

Carnivore Bulletproof Coffee is an energizing drink made with butter and beef fat. Perfect for mornings, it provides a creamy and satisfying boost to your day.

PREP TIME: 5 MINS

COOK TIME: 00 MINS

SERVING 1

INGREDIENTS

1 cup brewed coffee
1 tbsp butter
1 tbsp beef fat (tallow)
Sweetener of choice (optional)

INSTRUCTIONS

1. Brew a fresh cup coffee and ladle it into a powerful food blender.
2. Add butter and beef fat to the blender.
3. Blend on full power for 30 seconds until the coffee becomes frothy and well combined.
4. Ladle the coffee into a mug and add sweetener if desired.
5. Serve hot as a rich, creamy drink.
6. Enjoy the smooth and satisfying flavors of this carnivore-style coffee.

NUTRITION

CALORIES: 200, PROTEIN: 0G, CARBOHYDRATES: 0G, FAT: 22G,

SHOPPING LIST

Week 1 Shopping List
Protein Sources
- [ ] Ribeye steak: 4
- [ ] Ground beef: 1.5 lbs
- [ ] Pork belly strips: 2 lbs
- [ ] Eggs: 3 dozen
- [ ] Bacon: 2 lbs
- [ ] Chicken wings: 2 lbs
- [ ] Lamb shanks: 2 lbs
- [ ] Duck breast: 2
- [ ] Salmon fillets: 4 (6-oz each)
- [ ] Shrimp: 1 lb
- [ ] Lobster tails: 2
- [ ] Pork chops: 2 (8-oz each)
- [ ] Beef short ribs: 2 lbs
- [ ] Whole chicken: 1 (4–5 lbs)
- [ ] Scallops: 8 large
- [ ] Venison roast: 1 (2 lbs)

Dairy & Fats
- [ ] Butter: 2 lbs
- [ ] Beef tallow: 1 lb
- [ ] Cream cheese: 8 oz (optional)

Snacks & Miscellaneous
- [ ] Pork rinds: 1 large bag
- [ ] Bone broth: 4 cups (or bones to make homemade broth)

Week 2 Shopping List
Protein Sources
- [ ] Ribeye steak: 3
- [ ] Pork belly strips: 2 lbs
- [ ] Eggs: 2.5 dozen
- [ ] Bacon: 2 lbs
- [ ] Chicken thighs: 2 lbs
- [ ] Salmon fillets: 3 (6-oz each)
- [ ] Shrimp: 1 lb
- [ ] Cod fillets: 2 (6-oz each)
- [ ] Lamb ribs: 2 lbs
- [ ] Beef tenderloin: 1 (1.5 lbs)
- [ ] Duck liver: 1/2 lb
- [ ] Brisket: 2 lbs
- [ ] Pork cutlets: 1 lb

Dairy & Fats
- [ ] Butter: 1.5 lbs
- [ ] Heavy cream: 1 pint (optional)
- [ ] Cream cheese: 8 oz (optional)

Snacks & Miscellaneous
- [ ] Pork rinds: 1 large bag
- [ ] Bone broth: 6 cups (or bones to make homemade broth)

Week 3 Shopping List
Protein Sources
- [ ] Ribeye steak: 3
- [ ] Ground beef: 2 lbs
- [ ] Eggs: 3 dozen
- [ ] Bacon: 2 lbs
- [ ] Chicken wings: 2 lbs
- [ ] Salmon fillets: 3 (6-oz each)
- [ ] Lamb chops: 2 lbs
- [ ] Pork loin: 2 lbs
- [ ] Duck breast: 2
- [ ] Scallops: 8 large
- [ ] Lobster tails: 2
- [ ] Venison roast: 1 (2 lbs)
- [ ] Whole chicken: 1 (4–5 lbs)

Dairy & Fats
- [ ] Butter: 2 lbs
- [ ] Heavy cream: 1 pint (optional)
- [ ] Cream cheese: 8 oz (optional)

Snacks & Miscellaneous
- [ ] Pork rinds: 1 large bag
- [ ] Bone broth: 4 cups (or bones to make homemade broth)

Week 4 Shopping List
Protein Sources
- [ ] Ribeye steak: 3
- [ ] Pork belly strips: 2 lbs
- [ ] Eggs: 3 dozen
- [ ] Bacon: 2 lbs
- [ ] Chicken thighs: 2 lbs
- [ ] Salmon fillets: 3 (6-oz each)
- [ ] Shrimp: 1 lb
- [ ] Duck liver: 1/2 lb
- [ ] Lamb shanks: 2 lbs
- [ ] Lamb ribs: 2 lbs
- [ ] Pork belly roast: 2 lbs
- [ ] Beef short ribs: 2 lbs

Dairy & Fats
- [ ] Butter: 2 lbs
- [ ] Heavy cream: 1 pint (optional)
- [ ] Cream cheese: 8 oz (optional)

Snacks & Miscellaneous
- [ ] Pork rinds: 1 large bag
- [ ] Bone broth: 6 cups (or bones to make homemade broth)

1ST WEEK MEAL PLAN

	BREAKFAST	LUNCH	DINNER	SNACK
DAY 1	Carnivore Breakfast Sausage Patties	Grilled Ribeye with Garlic Butter	Slow-Cooked Beef Short Ribs	Bacon-Wrapped Sausage Bites
DAY 2	Beef Tallow-Fried Eggs	Pan-Seared Salmon with Lemon Butter	Roast Leg of Lamb with Pan Juices	Grilled Shrimp Skewers with Garlic Butter
DAY 3	Smoked Salmon and Scrambled Eggs	Butter-Poached Duck Legs	Whole Roasted Chicken with Tallow Rub	Crispy Pork Cracklings
DAY 4	Poached Eggs with Bone Broth Sauce	Lamb Ribs with Herb-Infused Butter	Filet Mignon with Duck Fat Gravy	Carnivore-Style Deviled Eggs
DAY 5	Duck Eggs and Crispy Bacon	Pan-Fried Pork Cutlets with Duck Fat	Grilled Swordfish with Bone Marrow Butter	Butter-Roasted Chicken Thighs
DAY 6	Butter-Basted Salmon Bites	Roasted Chicken Wings with Beef Fat Drizzle	Pork Belly Roast with Crackling Crust	Carnivore Egg Muffins
DAY 7	Egg and Cream Cheese Pancake	Bone Broth-Braised Lamb Ribs	Braised Oxtail in Beef Stock	Chewy Pork Rind Bites

2ND WEEK MEAL PLAN

	BREAKFAST	LUNCH	DINNER	DESSERT/BEVERAGE
DAY 1	Lamb Chop Breakfast Platter	Beef Tenderloin and Bone Marrow Plate	Grilled Salmon with Crispy Skin	Grilled Chicken Tenders
DAY 2	Creamy Scrambled Eggs	Crab Meat with Garlic Butter Sauce	Duck Confit with Crispy Skin	Butter-Basted Scallops as a Side Dish
DAY 3	Baked Eggs in Bone Broth	Grilled Sausage and Butter Dip	Venison Roast with Garlic Butter Sauce	Bacon-Wrapped Cheese Sticks
DAY 4	Grilled Sausage with Fried Duck Egg	Seared Cod with Beef Fat Sauce	Pork Loin with Butter Herb Glaze	Fried Pork Belly Cubes with Garlic Butter
DAY 5	Seared Beef Heart with Buttered Eggs	Smoked Brisket with Bone Broth Glaze	Lamb Meatballs in Bone Broth Sauce	Pan-Fried Sausage Bites
DAY 6	Easy Salmon Patties	Pan-Seared Lamb Chops with Garlic Butter	Slow-Roasted Lamb Shoulder	Hard-Boiled Eggs with Salted Butter
DAY 7	Beef Fat-Fried Chicken Thighs	Pork Belly Strips with Herb Butter Glaze	Grilled Lobster with Butter Dipping Sauce	Scrambled Egg and Pork Belly Mix

3RD WEEK MEAL PLAN

	BREAKFAST	LUNCH	DINNER	SNACK
DAY 1	Egg Custard with Heavy Cream	Lamb Shank Stew	Pan-Seared Scallops with Butter	Pork Belly Crisps with Beef Fat Glaze
DAY 2	Carnivore Panna Cotta	Pork Chops with Crispy Cracklings	Crispy Duck Wings with Tallow Dip	Carnivore Meatballs
DAY 3	Frozen Butter Bites with Vanilla Flavoring	Beef Bone Broth Soup	Roasted Bone Marrow and Garlic Soup	Butter-Fried Chicken Livers
DAY 4	Creamy Egg Pudding	hrimp and Crab Bisque (Dairy Optional)	Spiced Duck Broth with Egg Yolk Swirls	Smoked Salmon Rolls with Cream Cheese
DAY 5	Carnivore Omelet with Ground Beef	Smoked Brisket with Bone Broth Glaze	Whole Roasted Chicken with Tallow Rub	Lamb Meatballs with Beef Fat Drizzle
DAY 6	Keto Carnivore Ice Cream	Slow-Cooked Oxtail Soup	Creamy Salmon Chowder	Seared Scallops in Garlic Butter
DAY 7	Cream Cheese and Egg Soufflé	Lamb Shank and Bone Marrow Stew	Lobster Bisque with Creamy Butter Base	Crispy Chicken Wings with Butter Dip

4TH WEEK MEAL PLAN

	BREAKFAST	LUNCH	DINNER	DESSERT/BEVERAGE
DAY 1	Salted Caramel Egg Custard	Hard-Boiled Eggs with Salted Butter	Butter-Seared Venison Chops	Carnivore Egg Muffins
DAY 2	Salted Butter Fudge	Pan-Fried Beef Steak Bites	Grilled Swordfish with Bone Marrow Butter	Tallow-Basted Fried Pork Belly
DAY 3	Bone Broth Latte with Butter	Bacon-Wrapped Cheese Bites (Optional Dairy)	Slow-Roasted Lamb Shoulder	Carnivore Deviled Eggs
DAY 4	Whipped Cream Coffee	Roasted Chicken Wings with Beef Fat Drizzle	ork Loin with Butter Herb Glaze	Carnivore-Friendly Sausage Platter
DAY 5	Salted Beef Tea (Warm Broth Drink)	Smoked Salmon Bites with Cream Cheese	Braised Oxtail in Beef Stock	Scrambled Egg and Pork Belly Mix
DAY 6	Carnivore Milkshake	Pan-Seared Scallops with Butter	Whole Roasted Chicken with Tallow Rub	Butter-Basted Scallops
DAY 7	Carnivore Bulletproof Coffee	Pork Belly Soup with Crispy Fat Topping	Grilled Swordfish with Bone Marrow Butter	Crispy Duck Breast Bites with Savory Glaze

	BREAKFAST	LUNCH	DINNER	DESSERT/BEVERAGE
DAY 1	Poached Eggs with Bone Broth Sauce	Grilled Salmon with Bone Broth Reduction	Venison Roast with Garlic Butter Sauce	Fried Pork Belly Cubes
DAY 2	Baked Eggs in Bone Broth	Seared Beef Heart with Buttered Eggs	Filet Mignon with Duck Fat Gravy	Bacon-Wrapped Cheese Bites

CONCLUSION

As you reach the end of Super Easy Carnivore Diet Cookbook for Beginners, take a moment to appreciate how far you've come. Transitioning to a new way of eating takes commitment, and by embracing the carnivore diet, you've simplified your nutrition while taking control of your health.

With over 100 easy recipes, a 30-day meal plan, and structured shopping lists, this cookbook has equipped you with the tools to make this lifestyle sustainable. By focusing on just five ingredients per recipe, you've learned that great meals don't need complexity—just quality ingredients and simple preparation.

You may have already experienced benefits like increased energy, mental clarity, or improved well-being. Remember, this is your journey—listen to your body, experiment with new recipes, and make adjustments as needed.

Most importantly, celebrate your progress! Every step forward is a success. You're now part of a growing community seeking health and vitality through mindful eating.

Index

B

Bacon-Wrapped Cheese Bites (Optional Dairy) 89
Bacon-Wrapped Cheese Sticks 62
Bacon-Wrapped Sausage Bites 94
Baked Eggs in Bone Broth 25
Beef Bone Broth Soup 72
Beef Fat-Fried Chicken Thighs 17
Beef Steak Bites 98
Beef Tallow-Fried Eggs 18
Beef Tenderloin and Bone Marrow Plate 38
Bone Broth Latte with Butter 116
Braised Oxtail in Beef Stock 58
Butter-Basted Salmon Bites 20
Butter-Basted Scallops as a Side Dish 102
Butter-Fried Chicken Livers 85
Butter-Poached Duck Legs 35
Butter-Roasted Chicken Thighs 95

C

Carnivore Breakfast Sausage Patties 13
Carnivore Bulletproof Coffee 120
Carnivore Chocolate Mousse 112
Carnivore Egg Muffins 64
Carnivore Meatballs 84
Carnivore Milkshake 119
Carnivore Omelet with Ground Beef 14
Carnivore Panna Cotta 107
Carnivore-Style Deviled Eggs 68
Chewy Pork Rind Bites 61
Crab Meat with Garlic Butter Sauce 40
Cream Cheese and Egg Soufflé 111
Creamy Chicken and Egg Drop Soup 73
Creamy Egg Pudding 109
Creamy Salmon Chowder 78
Creamy Scrambled Eggs 19
Crispy Chicken Wings with Butter Dip 87
Crispy Duck Breast Bites with Savory Glaze 92
Crispy Duck Wings with Tallow Dip 42

D

Duck Confit with Crispy Skin 50
Duck Eggs and Crispy Bacon 22

E

Easy Salmon Patties 21
Egg and Cream Cheese Pancake 24
Egg Custard with Heavy Cream 105

F

Filet Mignon with Duck Fat Gravy 59
Fried Pork Belly Cubes with Garlic Butter 90
Frozen Butter Bites with Vanilla Flavoring 108

G

Grilled Chicken Tenders 96
Grilled Lamb Chops with Mint Butter 91
Grilled Lobster with Butter Dipping Sauce 57
Grilled Ribeye with Garlic Butter 29
Grilled Salmon with Bone Broth Reduction 100
Grilled Salmon with Crispy Skin 48
Grilled Sausage with Fried Duck Egg 26
Grilled Shrimp Skewers in Herb Butter 88
Grilled Shrimp Skewers with Garlic Butter 67
Grilled Swordfish with Bone Marrow Butter 52

H

Hard-Boiled Eggs with Salted Butter 63

K

Keto Carnivore Ice Cream 110

L

Lamb Chop Breakfast Platter 16
Lamb Meatballs in Bone Broth Sauce 55
Lamb Meatballs with Beef Fat Drizzle 65
Lamb Ribs with Herb-Infused Butter 41
Lamb Shank and Bone Marrow Stew 74
Lamb Shank Stew 32
Lobster Bisque with Creamy Butter Base 81

P

Pan-Fried Pork Cutlets with Duck Fat 39
Pan-Fried Sausage Bites 69
Pan-Seared Lamb Chops with Garlic Butter 99
Pan-Seared Salmon with Lemon Butter 30
Pan-seared scallops with butter 51
Poached Eggs with Bone Broth Sauce 23
Pork Belly Crisps with Beef Fat Glaze 70
Pork Belly Roast with Crackling Crust 56
Pork Belly Soup with Crispy Fat Topping 80
Pork Belly Strips with Herb Butter Glaze 97
Pork Chops with Crispy Cracklings 31
Pork Loin with Butter Herb Glaze 47

R

Roasted Bone Marrow and Garlic Soup 79
Roasted Chicken Wings with Beef Fat Drizzle 34
Roast Leg of Lamb with Pan Juices 46

S

Salted Beef Tea (Warm Broth Drink) 118
Salted Butter Fudge 114
Salted Caramel Egg Custard 113
Scrambled Egg and Pork Belly Mix 101
Seared Beef Heart with Buttered Eggs 27
Seared Cod with Beef Fat Sauce 43
Seared Scallops in Garlic Butter 83
Shrimp and Crab Bisque (Dairy Optional) 75
Slow-Cooked Beef Short Ribs 45
Slow-Cooked Oxtail Soup 77
Slow-Roasted Lamb Shoulder 53
Smoked Brisket with Bone Broth Glaze 33
Smoked Salmon and Scrambled Eggs 15
Smoked Salmon Bites with Cream Cheese 86
Smoked Salmon Rolls with Cream Cheese 66
Spiced Duck Broth with Egg Yolk Swirls 76

V

Venison Roast with Garlic Butter Sauce 54

W

Whipped Cream Cheese Mousse 106
Whipped Cream Coffee 117
Whole Roasted Chicken with Tallow Rub 49

Printed in Great Britain
by Amazon